Socrates: The Best of Socrates

The Founding Philosophies of Ethics, Virtues & Life

3rd edition

<u>Disclaimer Notice:</u>

Please note the information contained within this document is for educational purposes only.

Every attempt has been made to provide accurate, up to date and reliable complete information no warranties of any kind are expressed or implied. Readers acknowledge that the author is not engaging in rendering legal, financial or professional advice.

By reading any document, the reader agrees that under no circumstances are we responsible for any losses, direct or indirect, which are incurred as a result of use of the information contained within this document, including – but not limited to errors, omissions, or inaccuracies.

Table of Contents

Introduction

Wisdom begins with wonder. - Socrates

I want to thank you for downloading the book, "The Best of Socrates: The Founding Philosophies of Ethics, Virtues & Life".

This book describes the life and beliefs of Socrates, one of the most famous ancient Greek philosophers. He is known in history as one of the world's greatest teachers and writers. He sets an important example of how to live a virtuous life.

The teachings of Socrates may be old, but they are still meaningful today. In a world where it is easy to forget good virtues due to worldly desires, we all need to be reminded why it is important to preserve our morals, values, and virtues, even if other people seem to be getting more cynical and negative every day. Please feel free to share this book with your friends and family, and please take the time to write a short review on Amazon to share your thoughts.

Chapter 1: The Philosopher in the Agora

"I cannot teach anybody anything. I can only make them think." – Socrates

Socrates was a philosopher who lived in Athens during the time of the ancient Greeks, around 350 years before the Roman Empire conquered the Greek islands. According to historical accounts, his father was a sculptor or stonecutter and his mother was a midwife. Socrates later learned his father's trade and made his living the same way.

When he was not working as a stonecutter, Socrates spread his ideas as a philosopher in the market or *agora*, as it is called in Greek. His friends and disciples gathered around him to hear his thoughts, but unlike some of the other teachers who also called themselves 'philosophers,' he did not receive payment for his teachings. He did not wish to receive payment because he wanted to avoid being associated with fake philosophers who were in it for the money and power. To explain why Socrates did this, we need to understand the situation he lived in.

During that ancient period, Athens was known to have a democratic government, but their democracy is very different from the kind we know today. Since the Greeks lived in city-states where the population is not as large as a modern country, they did not need to elect representatives for the government. Instead, all male Athenians, were required to take part in government. Women, on the other hand, were not considered citizens, and were not allowed to take part in any area related to the government. Ironically, Athenian citizens had to be the sons of Athenian women.

A peculiar rule during that time was that they did not have lawyers, but had to defend themselves if ever they were accused of anything. The fake philosophers set up schools teaching rhetoric, or the art of discourse. The lessons here focused on being able to argue well for your side, or against the opponent's side. The goal is to win the argument regardless of the truth.

Because of this blatant disregard for the truth, those who view philosophy as a way to search for the truth began to call these false teachers rhetoric 'sophists.' The word for wisdom in Greek is sophia, so the term sophist has an ironic meaning. It highlighted the fact that these teachers were not teaching the truth, but how to bend the story to get away with a fault.

There were already a number of philosophers who were known in ancient Greece during Socrates' time, but most of these people focused on what was then called natural philosophy. This philosophy tried to determine the origins of the Earth and the universe. Socrates was one of the first who focused on virtue or moral living.

Socrates gained his followers by presenting a different view. He showed that it is desirable to live a life according to good virtues. He felt that the aim of philosophy is to care for the soul.

Since Socrates made fun of the sophists, it was to be expected that he would make some enemies. In time, they found something serious to accuse him of. He was said to be a critic of democracy and was guilty of teaching immorality. His defense for himself was described by Plato in "The Apology". It was there that he showed the faults of Athenian justice. In the end, Socrates was considered guilty. He accepted the sentence of death instead of escaping.

Most of the details of Socrates' life and beliefs were described by Plato in his Dialogues, leading to some people having difficulty differentiating between Socrates's ideas from Plato's. It became more difficult considering that Plato shared his ideas through the Dialogues where Socrates also took part in the discussion. To clarify this, we need to explain why Plato wrote in this way.

Both Socrates and Plato believed that a study of philosophy should encourage a student to think of himself. As such, Plato wrote his lessons in the form of Dialogues where characters based on real people exchange views on a chosen topic. The reader is supposed to imagine taking part in this discussion, albeit he is not able to say his thoughts, and come to his own conclusions. Although Plato had his own conclusions that were made obvious when one reads the Dialogues, the fictional discussion usually ends up inconclusive. For example, the participants admit that they cannot come up with a conclusive answer and may need more time to think about it. We must understand that the Dialogues do not necessarily describe actual discussions, although they may be based on actual events.

So how do we distinguish between Socrates' ideas and Plato's? Generally, most academics believe that the early Dialogues that talk about virtues describe Socrates' ideas. The later Dialogues that discuss more complex topics like knowledge and politics are considered to describe Plato's ideas.

Regardless of whether the Dialogues discuss Socrates' original ideas or Plato's, they express these concepts through what is to be known as the Socratic Method. This involves an exchange of questions and answers between those participating in the dialogue. During their discussion, Socrates' opponent ends up questioning his own initial beliefs.

The Socratic Method proceeds like this:

Socrates: What is X?

Other person: X is A, B, and C.

Socrates: Why is X A? Why B? Why C?

Other person: Because D, E, F.

This continues until everything that can be questioned about the other person's beliefs is asked. Of course, one uses logical reasoning to argue one's point and not simply rhetoric. Philosophy cannot be characterized by the use of emotions, flowery language, and other methods of rhetoric. It cannot support arguments based on fallacies. It must always follow the rules of logic and correct reasoning based on facts or the truth.

The Socratic Method is often referred to as a "dialectical method," or simply "dialectic." The term refers to a dialogue between two people. Socrates believed that conversation was the best way to conduct philosophical investigation (in fact, he was firmly opposed to the idea of philosophical writing: we'll explore this issue later in this book). The dialectic method is something that became a common philosophical instrument with later Greek philosophers, and endured all the way to the creation of the first European universities in Paris and Oxford during the Middle Ages.

But what was Socrates concerned with exploring during these dialectics, apart from simply encouraging his companions to question their beliefs? At the core of Socrates' philosophy is a desire to uncover the truth.

For Socrates, though, there was a difference between "truth" and "Truth." Today, philosophers distinguish between the two when analyzing Socrates' words (as they appear in Plato's dialogues). While Socrates was constantly in pursuit of "Truth" with a capital T--this was the underlying motivation of much of his philosophical inquiry--he felt that it was possible to make "true" statements along the way. The difference between "Truth" and "truth" for Socrates is difficult to elucidate, but it's an important distinction to make. "Truth" for Socrates meant perfect knowledge of something, and was his end goal whenever he chose to analyze a topic or an idea. As a means of reaching this ultimate end of "Truth," it was important to make use of logic, analyze simpler, less complex beliefs, and ensure that anything he took for granted along the way was, in fact, "true," and based in sound knowledge.

To further clarify this, consider Socrates' epistemology or his theory of knowledge. For him, knowledge is justified true belief. In other words, it is a true belief that has been given good reason for being true. This is a complex idea which requires a lengthy discussion because it is possible to disagree on what constitutes correct justification. Is it a logical argument? Is it having intense feelings connected to that belief? For Socrates and other philosophers, the correct justification has always been logic. No one who says his beliefs are true because he feels intensely about them has ever been considered a philosopher by the ancient Greeks.

What usually results from the Socratic Method is that a questionable belief is proved incorrect because the illogical reasoning or premises are uncovered. We need to keep this in mind when learning about Socrates' ideas. Even when this book lists down the most important lessons, to stay true to Socrates' wisdom, we still need to ask if Socrates' has indeed taught the truth. That way, we learn to think critically instead of simply accepting what other people tell us. After all, accepting blindly is the easiest way to believe in falsehoods.

Socrates' whole philosophical project was discovering the ultimate Truth in everything. He took very little for granted, and was constantly skeptical of people's commonly held beliefs and ideas. Over and over, he implored the people he conversed with to examine the things they assume to be true, and to accept the possibility that their deepest and most foundational ideas about the world might in fact by based in falsehood.

It's no surprise that Socrates had a mixed reception in his day: people clung to their beliefs in ancient Greece, just as they do today. Socrates made it his life's work to poke holes in those beliefs. Some people (such as Plato) admired him for this, and sought to learn from him. Others, as we'll see, turned against him.

Chapter 2: Socratic Beliefs

One can never undermine the contributions of Socrates to philosophy. It was his revolutionary perspective that went on to influence the future generations. His many philosophies have devolved into many cultures that have evolved in terms of thought process over the millennia. The predominant concept of Western thought has its roots in the philosophy propagated by Socrates.

Socrates was condemned by many as they felt that he was polluting the minds of the Athenian youth with thoughts that were capable of questioning the moral beliefs of the society at large. He earned the spite of many by questioning the moral values on which the society was built. Nevertheless, it was Socrates who gave us interesting and inquisitive theories that are not only fodder for the human brain but also for the conscience.

In this chapter, we identified the important beliefs of Socrates, ranging from theories, ideologies to his opinions about various things.

Before we move on to look at the various philosophical theories proposed by Socrates, there arises a need to understand the source of these philosophies. Since Socrates did not record his teachings anywhere, we are left with but no choice to refer to the literary works of his disciples, Plato and Xenophon. While there are other accounts of Socrates--other philosophers mention him in their writings, and his contemporary Aristophanes makes him a character in a number of his plays--it's his students' writings that tell us the most about him. Plato's *Diaglogues*, in particular, are our best source of information for what Socrates said and believed.

Plato's accounts of Socrates are mostly in the form of elaborate dialogues. For a reader, it is not possible to distinguish between the beliefs of Socrates and Plato. Hence, there have been many controversies that test the authenticity of the literary accounts of Plato in connection with Socrates. Nevertheless, no other source exists to verify the origin of all these beliefs that have been attributed to Socrates by his disciples. Let us now look at the various theories of Socrates in detail.

Sources

Our understanding of Socrates and his philosophies derive from a variety of historical sources. These sources are important, not just for the information they hold on the thoughts of one of the most influential thinkers of human history, but how others saw the man and his beliefs, as well as how that information was used in politics, arts, history, entertainment and other forms.

Philosophical and Literary Sources

During his lifetime, Socrates and his beliefs were often cruelly mocked, especially within plays. Indeed, many of the plays that refer to him have only survived in fragmentary form with *Clouds* being the exemption to this. In *Clouds*, Socrates was the main character, but Aristophanes, the author, did not show him in a balanced and realistic light (something comedy never does) but uses him instead as the representation of particular intellectual inclinations within Athens at that time, particularly of the study of languages, human nature and the morals and atheism, which goes hand in hand with them. When we look closer at *Clouds* as a dependable historical source for Socrates and his beliefs, it becomes less reliable when looking at Plato's *Apology*, when Socrates discards it as a lie.

When Socrates died, there were numerous friends and followers of his who began the task of recording his beliefs, ideas and character in various works, in particular, his conversations with others. The characters with which he was depicted conversing with were typically adversaries but also included those who supported his beliefs, political figures, philosophers, scholars and everyday people whom he came into contact with. Many of these works, however, have been lost but there are fragments written by Phaedro, Eucleides and Antisthenes, while Plato's and Xenophon's works have survived completely intact. As such, our main knowledge of Socrates and his beliefs originate from Plato and Xenophon (both their works were entitled, *Apology of Socrates* and centered on his trial). However, it should be noted that the majority of scholars believe that these works are not a reliable or accurate historical account of what Socrates said entirely. However, they are considered a general portrayal of what questions Socrates was asked, the way in which he responded and the overall philosophical direction that developed from those dialogs.

Xenophon

Out of the works of Xenophon, it is *Memorabilia*, which offers us a fuller portrayal of Socrates. The first two chapters of Book One center on the repudiation of the charges brought against Socrates at his trial and provide an addendum to his *Apology to Socrates*, which also centers on the same topic. However, in books Three and Four of *Memorabilia*, there is a distinct impression that he was influenced by Plato's works and so this diminishes some of the authenticity. Xenophon's *Symposium* (a work featuring Socrates conversing with friends at a party – which may have been inspired by a work of Plato's bearing the same title and subject) has often been believed to be an important recreation of how the philosopher lived and thought. Lastly, in Xenophon's *Oeconomicus* (meaning Estate Manager), he uses the various qualities he admired within Socrates to convey how one should manage a property. It was most likely not to have been a real conversation by Socrates.

Plato

Plato has often been exclaimed as one of the greatest philosophers throughout history, unlike Xenophon. It was his philosophical skillfulness which allowed him to understand the thoughts and dialogues of Socrates and, as a result, become a much more dependable source of knowledge regarding him. However, the contradicting theory is that Plato's skill and originality allowed him to utilize the Socratic dialogues, not just as a reproduction of those conversations, but also as a means of getting his own philosophies heard and recognized, even if they were inspired by Socrates. Therefore, this would mean that Plato's standing as a reliable and accurate source of knowledge regarding Socrates and his philosophies is far less than that of Xenophon's. However, whichever stance you take on it, it is clear that Plato was the one, which possessed far greater literary and philosophical skills.

Nowadays, philosophers who specialize in ancient Greek philosophy generally agree that there is a balance to be struck when analyzing Plato's accounts of Socrates. As mentioned in the last chapter, Plato's earliest dialogues--which feature Socrates discussing comparatively simpler ideas, such as the nature of virtue--are considered a relatively accurate source of information about Socrates' actual beliefs, theories, and ideas. Meanwhile, Plato's later dialogues--the ones in which Socrates begins to discuss more complex topics, such as the nature of knowledge, and to espouse various ideas in the realm of political philosophy--are considered to be more indicative of Plato's ideas than of Socrates'. It's important to remember, too, that Socrates and Plato had a very close student-teacher relationship. This would have looked very different from the way we envision a student-teacher relationship today.

To give you a sense of this, consider Aristotle and his students. Aristotle would become Plato's greatest student, and go on to write some of the most important foundational philosophical works in the Western canon. As Aristotle become an increasingly prolific philosophical author and gained notoriety in the ancient Greek world, he took on a number of students himself (just as Socrates and Plato had). Contemporaries of Aristotle would sometimes call his students "Aristotelians"; but, they just as often called them the "peripatetics." Peripatetic literally means "someone who travels from place to place." They called his students this because they literally followed Aristotle around everywhere. As he traveled from place to place, or simply walked about town, he would give philosophical lectures. A small band of his closest students would quite literally follow him, taking notes and trying to memorize his words as best they could.

It's easy to understand, then, how deeply indebted Plato's ideas were to Socrates'. Socrates had a much deeper impact on the formation of Plato's philosophical thought than the average teacher might have on a student today. So, even when we're unsure about whether an idea attributed to Socrates in Plato's works is actually 100% Socratic, it's still safe to say that there's some kernel of Socrates' ideas present.

Within the majority of Plato's woks, Socrates is the main conversationalist but there are a number of works where Socrates plays a smaller part (namely, the *Statesman, Parmenides* and *Timaeus*, all believed to be Plato's later works) and another work, *Laws*, where the philosopher doesn't appear at all. Why does Plato give Socrates a larger role in certain works and smaller ones in others? The general consensus is that Plato was attempting to indicate to the audience that the dialogues in which he is the chief conversationalist express Socrates personal philosophies and thoughts and in those where he plays a smaller role, or none at all, are Plato's personal thoughts.

However, there are a number of scholars who refute this theory, citing numerous reasons why so many academics do not agree. First, it is generally believed that Plato would not have given himself such a submissive part in so many of his works or just as a messenger of the thoughts of Socrates. In addition to this, Socrates seems to be incomprehensible in Plato's works; for example, in some works Socrates is the main converser, with himself stating that he cannot give a clear answer to certain questions such as "what is courage?" in *Laches*, or "what is piety?" in *Euthyphro*. But then in other works Socrates is given bigger parts and gives elaborate answers to certain questions. Within Books Two to Ten of *Republic*, Socrates offers his view of what an ideal society should be, the nature of the soul, what is reality and many other subjects. If we were to believe that Plato records all Socrates philosophies within his works – beliefs that were Socrates alone and with no influences added by Plato – then this would mean that Socrates holds both the answers and no answers to his own questions.

It is because of this that scholars are hesitant to hold these later works (including *Republic* and *Phaedo*) as reliable and accurate sources of information pertaining to the thoughts and philosophies of Socrates, even if they do feature a character bearing the same name and argue for particular values and against certain points. However, it is indicative that Plato used Socrates' name as a main character in his works to offer notions that may or may not have been expressed by the historical Socrates. As such, it is much clearer that Plato was expressing his own ideals and beliefs that came from his interactions with Socrates, utilizing examination and analysis methods from Socrates, which then allowed Plato to highlight what, could be achieved using these thoughts. It is these reasons, therefore, why Socrates is given larger roles in particular works, even though they were not meant to be a record of the great philosopher's thoughts and beliefs.

Consequently, the conversations of Plato which follow more accurately to what he listened to from Socrates are what the converser named Socrates looks to for answers to the questions of the nature of moral virtues and additional subjects (most of the time without coming up with a satisfactory answer) and can be found in *Laches* and *Charmides*, some of Plato's earlier dialogues. However, it should be noted that these conversations were not an entirely accurate dialogue, which Plato overheard of Socrates. We simply do not know how accurate or reliable these dialogues are or how much influence Plato had in shaping the material. Instead, we need to remember that Plato is simply reconstructing the general outline of conversations Socrates once had and presenting the methods, which Socrates utilized, and the expectations he had when questioning the ethics and morals of those he came into contact with.

The portrayal of Socrates in these works is similar to the one portrayed in Plato's *Apology*, another relatively early work of Plato's. Within the *Apology*, Socrates states that he doesn't question natural phenomena contrary to what Aristophanes charges. Instead, Socrates states that he is only concerned with one thing – how he and his followers can be good humans. The questions that he asks other people serve as a means of acquiring the wisdom relating to this. This corroborates with the Socrates we find in *Laches* and *Charmides*, but not within the *Republic* or the *Philebus*. As a result, we cannot be certain as to how much of the character named Socrates and the dialogues presented in these works are actually based on the historical figure of Socrates. In these works, the character, Socrates, has a method of analyzing what his conversers say and recognizes the foolishness within them due to seeing the illogicalities in their thoughts.

The term 'Socratic Method' is used as a label for an educational tactic where a student is cross-examined by their teacher. Yet this was not entirely accurate of the methods used by Socrates within Plato's dialogues. Instead, Socrates claims that he is just an oblivious inquirer, and asks certain questions, such as 'what is piety?' to others who possess no satisfactory answer. Socrates asks several questions to those he converses with, resulting in them having to retract their original answer because they do not corroborate with the answers to the additional questions. This strategy Socrates uses highlights that the converser has an inadequate understanding of the thoughts being debated. The other converser then, being disproven of the principles he originally stated, is able to give a new answer to the original question, or else a new character takes their place. However, even when these new answers are given, new inconsistencies are highlighted and ultimately Socrates obliviousness is shown as a sophisticated and deep sense of perception and the conversers are shown to be ignorant.

Nonetheless, it is important to realize that just because Socrates states that he is ignorant regarding particular subjects does not mean that he holds complete conclusions regarding every subject. Quite the reverse, since he possessed certain moral convictions, which he was completely confident about. When he delivers his defense speech to the judges, he states that wisdom begins when one recognizes that one is ignorant – an unexamined life is not satisfactory, that ethical virtue is above all else and that only by being good that you cannot be harmed (since virtue and morals will remain no matter what calamities may befall upon you). However, Socrates is also well aware that his thoughts on these subjects do leave some of the most significant questions relating to virtues and morals unanswered. It is therefore Plato's role to use the Socratic method to provide satisfactory answers to these enquiries.

Aristotle

Aristotle is one of our most important sources when it comes to the historical Socrates but, more importantly, he offers us additional proof of the method for highlighting the different philosophies or Socrates and Plato. Aristotle was 17 years old when Socrates had been dead for 30 years and settled in Athens specifically in order to study at Plato's school, known as the Academy. It is inconceivable that Aristotle had no conversations with those who had known and talked with Socrates. Therefore, scholars agree that the information Aristotle offers on the historical Socrates is actually founded on those dialogues. Aristotle claims that Socrates would ask questions but did not offer a response to them as he had no knowledge, that he was searching for characterizations of virtues and focused on moralistic subjects instead of being concerned with the natural world. The Socrates that Aristotle portrays is the same as Plato offers within his works and therefore makes it more reliable as a source.

Chapter 3: The Examined Life

"The unexamined life is not worth living." – Socrates.

When the jury proclaimed Socrates to be guilty and sentenced him to death, Socrates delivers one of the most significant statements to be spoken within philosophy. He states that "an unexamined life is not worth living for human beings" (*Apology*). Socrates persisted in his belief that we should reflect on what we do and say, acknowledge what we know and are ignorant about and look for ways to live a good, decent life.

This is, at its core, the central focus of Socrates' teachings. The notion that we as humans must examine our lives in order to discover our purpose was, as stated in the first chapter, quite a significant shift in ancient Greek philosophy. Rather than focusing on attempting to explain away the various phenomena in the natural world--as the so-called "natural philosophers" of Socrates' day attempted to do--or using philosophical argument for personal gain--as Socrates' enemies, the Sophists, chose to do--Socrates was focused on the importance of examining our lives, our ideas, and our beliefs in order to arrive at Truth, and improve upon who we are as humans.

A number of scholars highlight Socrates' stress on the nature of human beings here and argue that his notions of living an examined life derive from our human nature. It is natural for us to live our lives according to pain and pleasure, seeking out power, prestige and wealth; the same notions that the Athenians of Socrates' day were. Socrates was not proposing that everyone should be rejecting all of those calls, but instead to examine them to see whether they were truly worthy of the human soul. An examined life was to look within and around to determine what our motivations are and whether they had any true meaning or worth. If they did not hold any value, or were potentially harmful, then it is up to us to seek out the important things in life.

In virtually every instance where Socrates appears in Plato's early dialogues--the ones which most scholars agree most accurately portray Socrates' actual ideas--Socrates is engaged in using the Socratic method to encourage his interlocutors to examine their own beliefs. By asking them to examine their beliefs, he's ultimately trying to lead them to the realization that they may be living their lives in a way unworthy of a virtuous human being. This focus on the importance of seeking out Truth, of determining what a virtuous life looks like, and of ultimately being able to live virtuously shows up again and again in Socrates' conversations, even up to the last moments of his life.

When we examine the *Apology* we can see how Socrates looks at the lives of those judging him in his trial. By proclaiming the importance of an examined life after his sentence has been judge, Socrates himself become a judge, covertly accusing those who sentenced him that they did not live a life worthy of living. He claims that even after they kill him, they cannot escape from examining their own lives, and that by not examining their lives is neither good nor possible, and it is worthy to be a good human being.

This notion is a stark contrast with contemporary philosophers who claim that we should be leading ethical lives and that it isn't essential to ask the same questions that Socrates himself asked in order to be a good person. Today, we may say that to live a good life we should live a just life and it isn't necessary to continually debate what the nature of justice is. However, Socrates would not agree, not because of what may be considered unjust, but in that examining our lives will continue to be valuable to us as humans.

Unity of Virtue; All Virtue is Knowledge

In the *Protagoras*, Socrates claims that every virtue (including piety, courage and wisdom etc.) is all the same and offers several reasons for his belief. Socrates argues against the notion that you can be wise without self-control, because folly is the opposite of both restraint and wisdom. If they were really different then they would have different opposites, since two identical things wouldn't, logically speaking, have different opposites. As is, the opposite highlights that an individual can't be wise without self-control.

Of course, this argument means that Socrates does something called "equivocation." To "equivocate" means to declare that two things are, for all practical purposes, equal or identical. When he claims that "folly is the opposite of both restraint and wisdom," he is doing something called "equivocating on" restraint and wisdom. That is to say, he's claiming that restraint and wisdom share something in common, by virtue of the fact that they're both opposites of folly, and are nearly identical. It's also implicit in his argument--meaning, his argument also makes it clear--that he's claiming that a lack of self-control and folly are equivalent. His contemporaries could have pointed this out to him when he was arguing with them: they could have said, "But Socrates, you're claiming that folly and a lack of self-control are identical, and then saying that restraint and wisdom are identical, but you haven't proven any of these things. So, your argument is flawed from the start."

What's interesting to note here is that Socrates was one of the first philosophers--if not *the* first philosopher--in the Greek tradition to explore epistemology (the study of how we create and understand knowledge, or how we come to know things), virtue, what it means to live a good life, and so on. His contemporaries weren't familiar with this line of thought, and often had no response to his questioning, as is demonstrated in Plato's dialogues. This is part of why Socrates' thought is so important: while he may have committed some logical errors, and made some mistakes that his opponents could have (but didn't) pick up on, the important thing is that he *chose to begin this line of thinking*. He departed from Sophistry (the philosophers who taught rhetoric and argument for profit) and natural philosophy (the philosophers who focused on attempting to explain away natural phenomena in the world), and set his sights instead on a deep inquiry into human values, motivations, and our lives in general. This set the stage for hundreds of years of human inquiry to follow.

Socrates' theory that there is a "unity of virtue" ~~The theory~~ is occasionally put together with another theory that virtue is a type of knowledge, in that whilst beauty and strength, amongst others, can be of value to human beings they can also be harmful if not complemented by knowledge or wisdom. As such, if virtues are valuable then they are knowledge as qualities are not either harmful or valuable and only valuable when paired with knowledge or damaging when paired with foolishness.

No One Errs Knowingly/No One Errs Willingly

In *Protagoras*, Socrates claims that "no one errs knowingly". This is just one example of his intelligence. If someone does something wrong and fails to make it right, then this is an 'intellectual error' or it is because they are ignorant as to what is right. If someone knew was what right, then they would not have done wrong. If they do something wrong, they did it because they did not have the knowledge as to what was right and wrong at the time they did it. If they say they knew what they did was wrong at the time, they are considered mistaken because if they had really understood what they did was wrong, they wouldn't have committed the wrong originally.

Because of this, Socrates rejects the notion of *akrasis*, weakness of the soul, since no one makes mistakes willingly. On the surface, it may appear that Socrates is prevaricating between knowingly and willingly, but in *Gorgias*, Socrates states to Polus that tyrants possess the minimalist amount of power compared with others in the city since they don't do what it is they want to do. A tyrant's motivation is tainted with ignorance and to such a degree that the consequences of it will be harmful. On the other hand, the consequences of the one full of knowledge will be valuable.

All of this tells us a lot about what Socrates believed about human nature, the human "soul" (as he often refers to it), and our intrinsic motivations as human beings.

The most obvious implication here is that Socrates is firmly convinced that "evil" does not exist in the human mind--or, at least, not as we would typically conceive of it. From either a legal or a philosophical standpoint, we generally conceive of evil as something involving ill will: in other words, in order to be "evil," someone must have it in their minds that what they're doing will harm other people, and subsequently choose to commit said act regardless of those consequences. In fact, said person might opt to pursue this course of action specifically *because of* the negative effect it might have on other people.

In Socrates' mind, this isn't how humans operate. If someone does something wrong--whether it involves a complex moral issue, or a simpler, more mundane topic--it's a result of ignorance, or lack of knowledge. This tells us a couple of things about Socrates.

First, it makes it clear that Socrates believes humans are inherently good. In other words, humans are guaranteed to pursue "the good" in any given situation, so longer as we're aware of what "the good" actually is.

Second, it confirms the importance of "knowledge" for Socrates. Since knowledge is the one thing that allows humans to pursue the good and avoid error and evil, pursuit of knowledge is of prime importance for humans in virtually every situation.

This leads us to another of Socrates' fundamental beliefs: that humans seek out good whenever possible.

All Desire is for the Good

The notion just stated is that humans desire goodness. When someone commits an act in order to achieve something it is always done for the goal in mind. The harmful things that happen are not because of it, but because of something else. When a leader sentences someone to death, it isn't because they find it pleasurable, but because they believe it is necessary. As a result, the act is focused on the good because that was the motivation behind it.

There is a comparable account of this within *Meno*, that a person who wants negative things don't really know they are negative or harmful because if they did, then they wouldn't want them. Humans don't really want bad or harmful things but instead, desire the things they think will be good or valuable but in reality are negative. They desire valuable things even while they don't possess the wisdom of what is really valuable.

Of course, at this point, something rather obvious may have become clear to the reader. Socrates is talking an awful lot about "the good," versus things that are bad, evil, or harmful. But what exactly does he mean by "the good?" And, is it transferable across generations? Is Socrates' idea of what is "good" still relevant for us today?

In Plato's *Republic,* Socrates discusses "the form of the good," or the truest form of good available to man, with his contemporary Glaucon. He claims that while the good "is not being," it is "superior to [being] in rank and power," and it's what "provides for knowledge and truth." What's clear here is that Socrates is actually positing "the good" as something that exists in the external world. We tend to think of good as an adjective in the modern world. Something can be good, or it can be bad--but we don't think of something called "the good" that exists independent of other things

This is precisely what Socrates thought, however. According to Plato's account, he believed that something called "the good" had an actual physical form in our world, and could be understood and appreciated the same way that we come to understand "rank," or "power," or other concepts that seem to stand apart from actual physical things in the world.

It is Better to Suffer an Injustice Than to Commit One

In *Gorgias*, Polus becomes angry when Socrates tells him it is better to suffer an injustice than it is to commit one. Polus counters that it is wrong to commit a bad deed, but to actually experience something bad is actually far worse. Socrates then claims that if something is worse, then it exceeds in both immorality and pain. Because committing an evil deed is not worse than actually experiencing one then it can't exceed the pain in experiencing an evil deed. As such, it is better to endure a bad deed than to commit one.

This notion should be appreciated with the Socratic emphasis on the Care of the Soul. When you commit a bad deed, then you hurt or damage your soul, and thereby the gravest thing that could ever happen to you. Socrates claims that it is more appropriate to be punished instead of avoiding it since the castigation will cleanse or decontaminate the soul of this immorality. Some scholars have posited that Socrates was indeed guilty of "impiety" and "corrupting the youth," and that this widespread claim about the necessity of punishment may have been used against him by his contemporaries leading up to his trial.

Eudaimonism

The classical Greek word for happiness is *Eudaimonia*, which does not reference to a particular state but instead, refers to being a certain way. *Eudaimonia* means well-being, instead of the contemporary notion of happiness. Many scholars believe that Socrates had two notions of *Eudaimonia*: one, that an individual will seek happiness as a foundation for their actions, and two, that it is necessary to seek happiness as one's foundation for their actions. When this this put together with Socrates' notions of virtue, it has left us uncertain. It is possible that Socrates' notion of virtue is the same as his notion of happiness – by being virtuous you are happy, or that if you are happy you are full of virtue or even that if you are virtuous doesn't mean that you will be happy. In *Meno* it is proposed that knowledge of good things will lead the human soul to happiness. In *Gorgias*, Socrates states that it is those who are virtuous and combine it with wisdom who achieve happiness.

Here again, we see Socrates' focus on the importance of a virtuous life. Many scholars argue that Socrates' position in *Gorgias* is one of the most accurate reflections of what the philosopher actually believe. If this is the case, this further solidifies for us the fact that virtue and wisdom were Socrates' two most important pursuits, since these are the only means of achieving happiness.

Ruling is an Expertise

Socrates continues with the idea that ruling is the same as art or *techne*, in that both subjects need knowledge to thrive and do well. A wise ruler rules his kingdom in order for the good of the people and not themselves, just as a physician never treats a patient to full health for their own benefits. Whilst being a ruler, just as a physician, comes with many benefits (such as money), it is inconceivable that a ruler or doctor will not perform as well as they can for those under their care. Ruling a kingdom is done for the sake of the people and justice.

Coming from Plato's *Republic*, these concepts are probably more indicative of Plato's political philosophy than of Socrates'. Still, there are some other interesting things about Socrates' political beliefs worth examining.

Socrates was a staunch critic of democracy. This is surprising, since we think of ancient Greece as the birthplace of democracy. Socrates' focus on the importance of questioning our deeply held beliefs and of not taking things for granted also seems to fit with our modern understanding of democratic governance, and with the importance of public argument for the sake of the public good (after all, as they say: democracy dies in darkness).

Regardless, though, Socrates was not a fan of democracy. He believed that the general public was unfit to rule, and that only those who possessed adequate knowledge ought to be given the responsibility of voting and making decisions that impact the public at large.

It's easy to see, then, where Plato's notion of the "philosopher-king"--the ruler described above--comes from. Socrates was almost certainly instrumental in forming Plato's opinions about what an ideal ruler ought to look like. The philosopher-king, according to Plato, must practice philosophy (the word itself in Greek meaning "love of knowledge"), while also living selflessly: for the sake of the people and justice, as already mentioned.

Socrates and Irony

The subject of Socrates and irony has been brought up many times by scholars and has various meanings. One viewpoint a number of scholars subscribe to is that Socrates irony means he was trying to communicate the contrary meaning and this is something that many of his contemporaries would have interpreted Socrates' declaration of ignorance. Indeed, the way Socrates praises Euthyphro and states he will be his student is an example of Socrates' irony. While the natural conclusion a number of other scholars make is that *eironeia* was considered a way of concealing or deceiving the other party.

Indeed, many scholars have argued that Socrates may not have ever believed himself to actually be "ignorant," as he often claims he is. Instead, these scholars are of the opinion that Socrates used this ironic trope as a means of luring his contemporaries into a kind of conversational trap, and in order to rub their noses in their own ignorance. So, for example, when Socrates is engaged in a philosophical discussion, he will often first claim his own ignorance, and ask the person with whom he's conversing to illuminate the subject for him. As their conversation continues, Socrates is frequently asked for his opinion, but he refuses to give it, referring back to his own ignorance. Finally, by the end of their debate, his opponent will have made a fool of themselves, and it seems clear that Socrates' final claim of his own "ignorance" is actually a subtle jab at the nonsensical case made by his opponent.

Irony and Socrates is a tricky subject. In *Gorgias*, Socrates asks Callicles to be easy with him so that be able to learn more. In response, Callicles says that Socrates is being ironic. Thrasymachus also claims Socrates is being ironic when he professes that he doesn't know anything, or conceals his thoughts, on justice. This is a prime example of the scholarly opinion mentioned above.

Aristotle describes irony as an endeavor of self-depreciation; that it is the opposite of arrogance and that those who do participate in irony are doing so in order to avoid being arrogant. If this is the case, then Socrates was inclined to be modest. However, it's obvious that Aristotle venerated Socrates, which complicates the validity of his opinion here. In other words, Aristotle's definition may be colored by his own desire to make Socrates appear to be the modest, wise philosopher that he was believed to be by his followers. This is in sharp contrast to the picture that Socrates' accusers painted of him leading up to his trial.

Leo Strauss, a philosopher from the 20th century, states that Socrates' irony in that he declined to display his preeminence before others, especially those who possessed a poorer intellect to his, was a way of getting his point across to the few others who were on level with his intellect. As such, Socrates' irony was meant to disguise his real meaning.

One of the most famous lessons from Socrates is that we ought to examine our lives. As mentioned above, Socrates was against simply accepting what others say without thinking. Let us follow his example and ask why this is.

Without a doubt, it's easier to accept other people's ideas on how we ought to live our own lives. If we do this, we don't have to think. We don't have to study our beliefs and lifestyle to see if we are doing the right thing. In a world where we are offered countless philosophies, religions, lifestyles, and ideologies, it can be difficult to choose what is best for us, so we accept whatever our recognized teacher or leader says.

But what if what we are taught is a mistake? What if the way we live results in harm to ourselves and other people? Should we blame our teachers if something bad happens to us or other people because of what they taught us?

This seems like the logical answer. After all, as blind followers, we are only doing what we are told; and yet it is possible to ask this question: Can we not choose an alternate path?

There was a time when we must be told what to do because we are too young and too ignorant to know what is best. As minors, when we do something wrong, our parents or guardians are sometimes blamed because it is assumed they incorrectly taught us what is right and wrong. However, as adults, it is assumed that we can already think for ourselves and so if we do something wrong, we are blamed for it.

This is a very simple point explaining why we need to examine our lives. When we believe in falsehoods, we suffer whatever consequences occur because of our beliefs. However, it is usually never that simple. Sometimes it is difficult to see how our false beliefs lead to harmful consequences.

Let's consider this example: You believe that all who do not share your religion must be considered your enemies. At the very least, you are not allowed to befriend non-believers. At its worst, you are encouraged to harm them.

Let's say you have been living your life according to this unexamined belief. Though others have been encouraging you to be more tolerant of other beliefs, you refuse because you believe tolerance is immoral. What results then is you miss out on another perspective on life. You automatically assume that those who do not share your beliefs are enemies, and those who make you believe otherwise are also enemies.

Let's also say that you are able to compare your life with others who do not share your beliefs. You see that others seem happier in their lives and you start to think perhaps you may be mistaken, but still you insist on your beliefs.

Now let's consider the opposite: Imagine that you are extremely tolerant of others. You do not judge other people even if you don't agree with their lifestyles and ideologies. You say that everybody has the right to live as they see fit.

As a result, perhaps other people think you are crazy for tolerating immorality. They refuse to befriend you, but you still insist on your beliefs.

Given these two examples, who is correct?

If Socrates were alive, he would ask, "What do you think?"

The point being made here is we *live our lives*, not the teachers or philosophers who tell us how we ought to live. Whatever consequences we experience because of our beliefs are experienced by us, and no one else. Given that, is it not important to decide for ourselves how we ought to live?

One further point to make here is that the examined life must be constantly evaluated. It is tempting to think that we only need to examine our beliefs once and we are set for life. Actually, we will encounter new experiences and new issues we need to think about. We may find that we need to change our views according to new experiences and realizations. As we will see later in this book, this is one of the reasons that Socrates was opposed to the idea of writing down his philosophy. As ironic as it is, Socrates believed that we must constantly reexamine our lives if we're going to make any headway towards reaching the truth, and that the written word couldn't accomplish this for us. When we write something down, it's essentially frozen in time: it doesn't bend and adjust to our changing circumstances.

Going back to the examples above, it might have been easy to be intolerant of other religions because you lived in a town where everybody shared the same religion. Once new people moved in or once you moved to a more diverse town, you were forced to examine your old beliefs.

Also, it may have been easy to tolerant other beliefs while the people you know never did any morally questionable acts. Once you know of people whose beliefs allow them to do things that do not seem right or injure others, you were forced to examine if you should still retain your usual level of tolerance.

The examples above refer to the constant examination of our lives on issues of morality or other people's beliefs. However, the lesson of the examined life can also apply to issues of personal identity. For example, when we examine our life, we can ask why we choose our current job, why we are friends with someone, why we love someone, and so on.

When we examine our life this way, we will know if our choices are the best for us according to who we are. Perhaps our current career is not maximizing our talents. Perhaps we are not as happy as we can be with the kind of friends we have. Continuously examining our choices encourages us to be critical thinkers and not fall into a rut. It encourages us to seek what is truly best for us.

Socrates truly paved the way with this kind of thinking. Rather than focusing on philosophizing about the natural world, Socrates turned his attention to virtue, wisdom, happiness, and the value of human life. This was an incredible turning point in the history of Western philosophy, something that can't be emphasized enough. Without Socrates' shift, the centuries of philosophical ethics (the study of what it means to live a moral life), epistemology (the study of how we create knowledge), and other important branches of philosophy wouldn't have been possible.

This point brings us to the next important lesson.

Chapter 4: Know That You Know Nothing

I am wiser than this man, for neither of us appears to know anything great and good; but he fancies he knows something, although he knows nothing; whereas I, as I do not know anything, so I do not fancy I do. – Socrates

This seems paradoxical. In the previous chapter, we say that we should examine our life to know what is best for us, but now Socrates encourages us to accept that we know nothing. So which is it?

To understand this point, we need to put it into context. The above quote is from "The Apology" where Plato describes Socrates' defense of himself after he was accused to be an enemy of Athens. In his speech, he described how a friend of his visited the temple of Apollo, and asked the oracle if there is anyone who is wiser than Socrates. The oracle answered that there is no one wiser than him.

When Socrates heard this, he did not believe it because he knew that he did not know anything. He tried to disprove the oracle by searching for someone wiser than him in Athens. In his search, he learned that other people claim to be wise, but in fact they are not. Politicians claimed to be wise even if they did not know anything. Poets claimed that their poetry expressed the truth even if they only made up the meaning of their words. The Sophists, perhaps worst of all, claimed to be wise and sold their supposed "wisdom" to others for a profit. Gradually, Socrates realized that the oracle meant he is wise because he knows he is not wise and does not pretend to be so.

The point of this lesson is that we need to accept that humans are imperfect creatures. Even if we have examined our beliefs as thoroughly as we can, it is still possible to misinterpret these beliefs. Human beings, even the most intelligent among us, are not God. We can always make mistakes.

We see here some kind of checks and balances to avoid going into the extremes. By only accepting the lesson of examining life, it is easy to think that just because we have examined our beliefs, they are already necessarily true. Or else, we might think that just because we constantly examine our beliefs, we are automatically wise.

We must be careful of this tendency. Going back to the example above, let us say that the belief in a lack of tolerance for other religions was accepted after much examination. As we have seen it is possible to experience needing to live amongst those who have different beliefs. If we think we are already wise with our beliefs because we have already previously examined them, then we might be too proud to consider an alternative perspective.

A lesson in humility is connected to this. This becomes especially applicable for people in positions of power or influence, especially when one has many followers. They should follow the example of Socrates, who never forces his friends to accept his views, but instead encourages them to think for themselves.

Now we need to be careful that we do not get into extremes when accepting that we know nothing. Though we are prone to make mistakes, this does not mean we should give up in trying to know the truth as Socrates encourages us to. We can seek the truth, but still be humble enough to know that we can misinterpret ourselves.

What Socrates is really getting at here is actually quite simple. In saying that we must acknowledge that we "know nothing," Socrates is encouraging us to start from the absolute beginning in our pursuit of knowledge on any particular topic. Generally speaking, when we investigate or study something, we begin with an enormous amount of intellectual baggage. We might have a high opinion of ourselves, or believe that we already know nearly everything there is to know on the subject, and just need to learn a little bit more. As we read (or in Socrates' case, as we have a discussion with another person), we constantly encounter information that may contradict our pre-existing understanding of whatever it is we're looking into.

If we refuse to let go of these pre-existing beliefs, we won't be open to the actual pursuit of truth. Instead, we'll be far too busy worrying about how to justify our existing beliefs in the face of contradictory information. This is especially true when another person is involved. It's one thing to encounter something in writing that challenges what you currently believe to be true; but, it's even harder to have someone tell you in conversation that you may be wrong about what you currently believe.

Socrates saw all of this, and felt that the best way to pursue *actual truth and knowledge* was to start with a blank slate. Dispense with all of your preconceptions, admit that you know nothing, and only *then* should you proceed with any inquiry.

Of course, while this is easy to understand, it's harder to do in practice. After all, once you've completed an inquiry, what do you do with the new knowledge you're supposed to have gained? How do we reconcile the need to cast aside our knowledge, claiming that we "know nothing," with the fact that we're supposed to have discovered at least *something* in any pursuit of truth?

For Socrates, the answer is that our search for truth must be constant. We constantly examine our lives and our beliefs. We constantly think. We never allow ourselves to become stagnant with dogma. Our minds are constantly evolving depending on new experiences.

Yet, if so, then does this mean we will never know the truth? Does this mean that perhaps the truth is relative? If people arrive at various conclusions after examining their beliefs, then are there many correct solutions to a problem?

These are complex philosophical questions that cannot be discussed in a short book. The important point is that Socrates encourages us to think for ourselves and to keep thinking. Just because we cannot be absolutely sure of the truth does not mean we should choose ignorance. In the same way, just because we cannot ensure that the world will forever be peaceful does not mean we should choose conflict. Just because we cannot always be healthy does not mean we should give up entirely on living healthy.

This brings us back to Socrates' idea of philosophy as the care of the soul. Here is one major difference between Socrates and Plato. While Plato went on to create a philosophical system, Socrates viewed philosophy with a more practical approach.

Socrates' claim that he "knew that he knew nothing," and his focus on a more practical philosophy, is important when we consider his complete lack of written philosophy. For someone who had such a profound impact on philosophy—and on the future of Western thought—one of the most interesting things about Socrates was his complete refusal to commit anything to writing. A shining example of this is in Phaedrus, when Socrates is asked why he's never written any of his ideas down on paper, to preserve them and carry them forward. Socrates replies that trying to write things down is "inhuman," because it's just an attempt to "establish outside the mind what in reality can only be in the mind." What is Socrates saying here, and what does this mean for us today?

As we saw in the last chapter, Socrates is famously quoted as saying that "the unexamined life is not worth living." He clearly believed that one of the most important things we can do is constantly question ourselves: our lives, our motivations, our relationships, our surroundings—everything. Leave no stone unturned. This is how Socrates lived his life, until the day he died. In fact, he was given the option after his trial of leaving Athens, rather than drinking hemlock. But his convictions were so strong and unshakeable that he chose to stick with what he believed— that it's important to question everything, whether or not that means you'll be accused of "corrupting the youth"—rather than take the easy way out.

Socrates never got involved in politics because he believed that he had no right to determine for others how they ought to live their lives: he said he was still trying to figure that out for himself first. This is exactly what he was getting at when he opted not to write down his thought. He believed that his job was to impress upon people the importance of their own path to truth—that they must seek out truth for themselves. If he wrote down his truth, trying to "establish outside the mind" the truths that he had realized for himself, it would mislead people. It would discourage them from examining their own lives. It would be, as he said, "inhuman."

Perhaps most importantly, it would violate his belief that he "knew nothing." Rather than commit something to writing, attempting to fix temporary understanding into something permanent, Socrates believed it better to constantly pursue new understanding. He made a point to daily cast aside his extant beliefs.

Socrates chose not to compose great philosophical works. He chose instead to live a simple life, one that involved the constant examination of everything that those around him took for granted. In doing so, he hoped to set an example for all of us: to never stop questioning until we arrive at the truth, and to always remind ourselves that true knowledge means admitting that we "know nothing."

Chapter 5: Uncovering the Socratic Method and Putting It Under the Scope of Examination

Developed from the dialogues of Plato, the Socratic teaching method may be defined as a student oriented approach that has the aim of challenging learners to develop their critical thinking skills as well as actively engage in discussion that is analytic. The Socratic Method may well be applied at any grade level and in any field of education.

Brief History of the Socratic Method

It is important to note that the Socratic Method, also called the dialectic method, is more than 2,400 years old. His opinion on lectures was strong and negative and he deeply believed that all lectures did was put a cap on the thinking ability of students. As per Matthew Copeland, Socrates held in high value the knowledge and content already in people's minds and he believed that if applied, the knowledge would be extremely useful in multiple contexts. Socrates believed, in the formation of his famous method, that by helping the student body examine any premonitions and beliefs that they had while at the same time accepting that the human mind was limited, their skills of reasoning could be sharpened to a high standard and they, would be able to flow from logic to logic with marked ease.

Lectures in Socrates' day looked nothing like the Socratic Method that he was developing. Students were discouraged from participating; rather, they were expected to sit quietly and absorb information from their teacher without questioning it. One can imagine how infuriated Socrates must have been by this, given how important he considered questioning our beliefs to be. He created his own method·of inquiry, using a dialogue between two or more people as a means of pursuing truth.

The term "Socratic Seminar" appears to have been first used by Scott Buchanan, the Great Books founder and since then, this concept has been popularized by multiple centers and organizations all over the world.

The Educational Aspect of the Method: Does Discipline Actually Matter?

If you take the utmost classic form of the Socratic Method, you will find that it uses creative questions to dissect, and with the same motion, ignore the current ideas in existence. This in turn allows the student to think about vital concepts in a completely new light, expanding his or her ability to think critically and basically opening new doors that he or she did not know existed. When it comes to questions that have a philosophical and expansive nature to them (for example, what is beauty? What is confidence? Is there a difference between courage and bravery?), the Socratic Method is phenomenal and is easily applied in solving these phenomena. However, when it comes to concepts that embody a clear definition, the method is not suitable. For example, the method will not help you much in answering the question "what is a cell?".

Based on this piece of information, we may well conclude that in some disciplines more than others, the Socratic Method is a lot more effective in answering questions. In subjective principles like philosophy, the humanities and art, the method works almost flawlessly. For objective disciplines such as Mathematics and multiple fields of science, this method is not as effective. This isn't surprising, considering the topics that Socrates chose to concern himself with in ancient Greece. Recall that he cared nothing for "natural philosophy," or the attempt to make sense of the minutiae and detailed workings of the world around him. Rather, Socrates was focused on more abstract lines of inquiry related to how we ought to live our lives. For this, the Socratic Method is ideal.

The Socratic Method of Teaching With Regard to Objective Disciplines

In the times that Socrates taught, the subjects of his time were not disciplined in quite the same way as they are in the modern day and age. During his time, mathematicians were known to don kitchen hats and explore cooking, just as the literature men would immerse themselves in philosophy for days on end. Compared to modern day academia, the boundaries were not as clearly and rigidly defined in his day and age. For these particular reasons and multiple others as well, Socrates was able to use his Socratic Method in multiple fields from philosophy to science and mathematics.

In recent times, a staunch student of the school of Socrates brought the method to an elementary school classroom. He made a habit of arriving on Friday afternoons, when the students were going berserk with impatience, and successfully taught them about place values using this method. He made clear their importance and why it was so vital to apply them. He confessed that this concept was a far cry from what the students were accustomed to in their math classes, but by careful implementation and consistently asking questions that were followed by more questions, he was successful in meeting his objectives and helping his students expand their way of thinking.

There's a bit of irony here, of course: when reading some of Plato's earliest dialogues (where Socrates is probably most accurately represented), especially *Gorgias*, Socrates is often represented as though he's conversing with children, rather than fellow adults. His interlocutors are stubborn and impatient, much the way that these elementary school children were. His use of the Socratic Method to tease out their preconceptions and attempt to lead them to new, untainted knowledge was not unlike the situation faced by a teacher in a classroom of children.

The Potential Difficulties With Regard to the Socratic Method

Basically, the Socratic Method involves tearing down old ideas and promptly replacing them with fresh concepts and ideas. For example, rather than discuss how to apply justice in social settings that are diverse and consistently changing, the students may discuss the very concept of justice itself. By going into deep dialogue and discussing this concept, with adept guidance from the facilitator, the students are able to discard whatever notions they may have had before and replace them with ideas that, in every sense, are truly philosophically savvy. Perhaps, the main problem that may come by using the Socratic Method is just how to handle the sheer diversity of the responses that arise from questions. What is even more unfortunate is that the way Socrates approached this problem and dealt with it has all but gotten lost in the immense folds of history.

For Socrates, this kind of potential divergence wouldn't have been seen as a problem. In fact, it would have been welcomed. In some cases, it may have been the entire point of the discussion. This runs against the current of most modern educational planning, where a syllabus is created with specific topics and outcomes, and standardized tests are used to measure success. Socrates would have opposed this kind of an approach to education, opting instead to embrace the diversity and uncertainty that can emerge from using the Socratic Method.

Putting the Modern Socratic Method Under the Scope

The modern version of the method rarely puts any reliance on the answers that the students give to a particular question. Rather, it places reliance on a particular set of questions that have been carefully designed so that they serve the purpose of leading the students to an idea. By using questions in consistent form, the teacher has the chance to get the class lively and excited. By making sure he starts with questions that he knows the students are familiar with, the teacher is able to help his or her class understand and internalize new concepts. This serves to create an atmosphere where the students are indeed learning as opposed to one where the student body merely parrots information and tries to cram as much of it in their heads as possible.

The Socratic Method cannot be said to be perfect for every discipline there is as well as in all classroom settings. However, it is a highly advantageous method that will serve to help the students in truly learning, as opposed to repeating information that may not make sense to them.

Socrates believed that knowledge was inborn, and could be accessed equally in all of us. Rather than focusing on memorization, or encouraging students to simply internalize what their teachers had to say, Socrates was focused on bringing out this inborn knowledge. By doing so, he believed that students could access "truths." While this approach to the dialectic method makes different epistemological assumptions than our modern approach, there's still a lot to be learned from it. Instead of operating on the assumption that the teacher in a classroom is the only person with knowledge to contribute to a lesson, the ancient Socratic Method assumes that, in fact, all of the students have an innate knowledge to bring to bear, too.

With the Socratic Method, classrooms can be transformed into places where everyone contributes, students and teacher participate equally, and the production of knowledge is democratized. This is what Socrates wanted to get at: the notion that students are responsible for arriving at their own conclusions, and should be prompted to pursue truth of their own volition. Rather than leaving a classroom with a fixed amount of information that they've gained from the teacher, the Socratic Method trains students to *think in a certain way*. This newly developed skill in critical thinking will serve the students for years to come, as they encounter new and challenging circumstances in their lives. The students will be able to think for themselves instead of regurgitating knowledge.

Chapter 6: Philosophy-The Way of Socrates & Philosophical Beliefs

Elenchus (Ancient Greek elengkhos: argument of disproof or even refutation; cross-examination, testing or scrutiny, especially for the purpose of refutation) is the core technique in the Socratic Method. Its Latin form, which is elenchus (plural, elenchi) is the technical philosophical term in English.

In the earlier dialogues of Plato, Socrates uses elenchus in his investigations; for instance, the very nature or even definition of such concepts of ethics such as justice and/or virtue. As per Vlastos, the elenchus of Socrates took the following steps in structure:

The debater of Socrates asserts a particular thesis; for instance, "courage may be defined as the soul's capacity to express endurance", a definition that Socrates considers utterly false and promptly targets for the process of refutation. Socrates moves on to secure the agreement of his interlocutor to further premises; for instance, "courage is indeed a fine thing" and "endurance of the ignorant kind is not a good thing at all".

Socrates follows this up with an argument, with the interlocutor agreeing that these premises that Socrates has brought on board very much imply the opposite of the original thesis that he expressed. In this case, it surely leads up to, "courage is certainly not endurance of one's soul". Socrates then claims that he has proven that the thesis of his interlocutor is devoid of truth and that its negation is indeed what is true.

One examination of the diverse kind may well lead to a brand new, much more refined examination of the concept that is being considered. In this particular case, what it does is invite a thorough examination of the claim "courage is indeed wise endurance of one's soul". The thing is with most Socratic inquiries, a series of elenchi crop up, eventually leading up to a sense of puzzlement that is known as aporia.

Frede himself points out that Vlastos conclusion in the last step, which is step 4, makes utter nonsense of that aporetic nature that was a key component in the early dialogues. Having ascertained that the proposed thesis is devoid of truth and is insufficient to conclude that some other competing thesis does indeed hold some truth to it, rather, what has happened here is that the interlocutor has reached aporia, an improved state, yet one of still not comprehending what to say exactly of the subject that is being discussed.

The very nature of the elenchus is subject to heavy debate. In particular arguments that gravitate around whether it is indeed a positive method that is usable in the stacking of knowledge or simply a negative method whose sole use is to refute false claims without necessarily adding anything.

Socrates was accustomed to saying that he himself "did not know anything" and that the one way he was wiser than the rest was via the recognition of his own ignorance first. It stands to reason, then, that leading his interlocutor to a state of aporia may indeed have been Socrates' entire purpose. He wasn't trying to lead his partner in conversation to a particular conclusion; rather, he wanted to instill in the other person an equal awareness that they ought to "know that they know nothing." They'd begin the conversation with an incredibly firm and steadfast belief in a particular bit of knowledge; but, by the end of the dialectic, they'd be forced to recognize that, in fact, they're unsure of what they can or cannot believe.

The Application According To Socrates

Generally, Socrates tended to apply his examination method to those concepts that appeared to lack any deep and defined definition. For instance, Socrates scope of examination was heavily focused on the key concepts of morality at the time- the important virtues, temperance, wisdom, courage and justice. Such an examination targeted the moral beliefs that the debaters heralded, raising up any inadequacies as well as inconsistencies whatsoever in their beliefs and eventually leading up to aporia. It is in view of such stark inadequacies that Socrates himself claimed ignorance and a lack of knowing, while others still professed knowledge and enlightenment. Socrates firmly believed that it was his acceptance of ignorance that made him far wiser than folk who still believed they knew but did not. At first glance, this belief appears to be paradoxical, even a little absurd. Yet, it was via this very belief that Socrates discovered his own errors, where others might have presumed correctness. The Delphic oracular pronouncement puts it forth that Socrates was indeed the wisest of all men that have lived, or rather that no man raised his bar of wisdom to the level that Socrates raised his own.

Socrates actively used this very claim as the core basis of his own moral exhortation. Socrates also claimed that the chief goodness lay in the painstaking caring of one's soul where moral truth is concerned as well as moral understanding. He also claimed that wealth is not the bringer of goodness but rather goodness brings wealth as well as all other blessings both to an individual and to his state. Socrates went ahead and expressed that life without dialogue, or examination in this case, was a life that was not worth living. It is with these beliefs in mind that the Socratic Method is deployed. For Socrates, then, the Socratic Method is the key to pursuing a just, virtuous life worth living: the "good life." Only through constant examination, and by pointedly avoiding assumptions and aiming to delve deeply into all aspects of our lives, can we reach the ultimate goal of living our lives according to Socrates' definition of excellence.

The motive present in modern usage of the Socratic Method and that of Socrates own particular use is not necessarily equivalent. Socrates rarely ever used the method in the development of theories. Rather, he employed myth to explain these theories.

The dialogue of Parmenides depicts Parmenides employing the Socratic Method to fish out and point out the flaws existing in the Platonic "theory of the forms", as presented by the philosopher Socrates himself. If anything, it is not the only dialogue in which those theories compounded by Socrates and his main disciple Plato are broken down via dialectic. Instead of arriving at specific answers, the method was employed in the breaking down of the theories that we hold, to travel beyond those hypothesises and maxims. The element of myth and the Socratic Method are in no way meant to be incompatible. The purposes they hold are not similar and they are often defined as the left and right hand paths to wisdom and overall good.

The Socratic Circles

You can describe a Socratic circle as a tutorial approach that has a firm grounding on the Socratic Method and employs a dialogic form approach to understanding and digesting the information presented in a text. The systematic approach it employs is used to examine a particular text via questions as well as answers embedded in the belief that all "new knowledge may trace its roots to prior knowledge or wisdom". It works on the basis that knowledge stems from asking questions and that one question asked should stimulate more questions being asked. By all means, the Socratic circle does not take the form of a debate or argument- rather, the entire body of learners is supposed to work together constructively and arrive at answers rather than having one of the learners score a "victory" in the argument.

The approach of the Socratic circle is based on the belief that if participants engage in meaningful and respectful dialogue, as opposed to memorizing blocks of information that has already been provided for them, they will gain a lot more understanding of concepts that may be drawn from the text.

This is an important distinction to make. Often in the modern world, we take the dialogic form of the Socratic Method to imply a kind of competition: two people engage in a dialogue, and one of them turns out to be "right," the other "wrong." This was not Socrates' approach at all, however. The purpose of the dialectic is not to prove or disprove a particular point; rather, it's to explore all possibilities, with both of the participants in the conversation eventually reaching a new level of understanding. Were the focus of the conversation to be on one person being "right," this would imply a pre-existing awareness of what's correct and what's not. In other words, it would run in sharp contrast to Socrates' position that he "knows that he knows nothing." There is, perhaps, much to be gained in our modern world (full as it is full of conflict) from adopting the Socratic approach to dialogue.

While the circles of Socrates may well differ in how they are structured and perhaps even in the naming, they will typically involve these components: a text passage that all students are expected to read beforehand and then two concentric circles that are made up of students i.e. an outer circle and an inner circle.

First, the inner circle plays the role of carefully examining and discussing the text while the 2nd circle, which is the outer circle, examines the heft and quality of the dialogue in question. Then the two circles swap places, as well as roles and the process itself is repeated with brand new ideas from a brand new circle.

While the inner circle reacts and follows the reaction with dialogues, the outer circle is expected to maintain a keen silence. Likewise, the inner circle is expected to be keen and attentive while the outer circle evaluates the conversation that has taken place.

A wise soul described Socratic circles, and their role in the class as follows; "Socratic Circles turn partial classroom direction, classroom control, and classroom governance over to the student body by equating what is frankly an equitable environment of learning where the mettle and heft of the students' voices and the voices of their teachers are just about indistinguishable from one another. In class, the Socratic circles help to stimulate critical, forward thinking that in turn will stimulate the growth of upstanding, responsible and productive citizens".

The Various Approaches to Socratic Circles

Different teachers tend to use Socratic circles in different ways. In each classroom, the structures may take a different approach. The list below is by no means exhaustive, but it is expansive enough that teachers may use any of these structures in the administration of a Socratic Seminar. By using these methods, teachers can open their students up to the possibilities inherent in the Socratic Method. Students who haven't responded to traditional pedagogical methods can be brought to life, and encouraged to participate in the classroom as a whole.

Here are the various structures:

The Inner/Outer Circle of the Fishbowl

In this structure, the students need to be arranged in two circles, an inner circle and an outer circle. The inner circle will have active engagement in discussion about the particular text in question. The outer circle, during this time, will observe the inner circle as they take notes and avoid all forms of interjection. The outer circle will then examine the argument or discussion of the inner circle and raise any concerns and questions that may arise under the guidance of their tutor or facilitator. The students will then employ constructive criticism, rather than go down the judgement road. The students that are present in the outside circle will keep a keen track of the topics that they feel they would like to discuss or dialogue on as part of their debrief to the class. The participants present in the inner circle may also use notes or an observation checklist to actively monitor the outer circle's participants. These tools will serve to provide the structure for listening as well as give the outside members specific details that will be taken up for discussion later on in the seminar. The teacher is welcome to sit in the circle. The catch here is that he or she must sit at the same height as his or her students.

The Triad

The students are usually arranged in such a way so that every participant (going by the name of "pilot") within the inner circle has three co-pilots that sit behind him on both sides. Pilots are the speakers in that they are placed in the inner circle. The co-pilots, present at their stations in the outer circle will only speak upon consultation. As such, they are not supposed to interject or interrupt the flow of discussion emanating from the inner pilot circle. There is no difference whatsoever in how this particular seminar moves forward as compared to other seminars. It will roll on just as its counterparts do. At a specific point in the seminar, the facilitator will stop the discussion and actively encourage the triad to talk to one another. The conversation will revolve around those topics that have established themselves as needing more in depth discussion or perhaps a question that the leader or facilitator has posed to his audience. At times during the conversation, a co-pilot may swap seats with a pilot and in doing so, swap the various roles they each play. Only then is the switching of seats tolerated. You may not just switch seats randomly because you have lost patience with the particular role you are playing. This unique structure allows those who may lack confidence to speak up in the large group a chance to voice their opinions and points.

The Simultaneous Seminars

Here, the students are arranged in many smaller sized groups and they are positioned as far as is possible from each other. Following the guidelines present in the Socratic Seminar, the students will then engage in small group discussions. The simultaneous seminars are usually done by students with sufficient experience who require little to no guidance and may engage in dialogue or discussion with no help from the facilitator or tutor. As per relevant literature, this seminar type works beautifully for those tutors who want their students to engage in the exploration of a variety of texts that have one main issue as their anchor. Each group may be allocated a different text to read and draw points from. After this, a larger Socratic Seminar may then be conducted with the main discussion being how the various blocks of text correspond with one another. Where the texts in question are difficult and pretty much too complex to simply pick at via a simple Socrates seminar, simultaneous seminars may provide a solution for these. It matters little what particular structure the tutor will go on to employ. The one basic premise of the seminars is to turn over partial governance and control over to the student body. The seminar serves to encourage the students to work together in deciphering meaning from the text as well as staying away from any pre-supposed "right" interpretation. The emphasis here is on critical thinking; thinking along creative lines.

We have talked quite a bit about texts to be read and where points are to be drawn from but we have not looked at how to select Socratic circle texts. We will look at that in the next section.

Selecting Texts

Texts used in the Socratic Circle

A Socratic circle text may be described as a document of the tangible kind that serves to create a thought provoking argument or discussion. The text, at all times, ought to be so that it is appropriate for the current degree of social and intellectual development of the participants at hand. It provides a firm spine for the dialogue, so that the tutor or facilitator is in a position to draw the class back to the relevant subject if he or she realizes that they have begun to digress. Also, the selected text enables all those who are participating to generate a level playing field. What this accomplishes is to ensure that the tone of dialogue remains straight and pure to the subject at hand without digression or even the element of distraction. There are practitioners of the Socratic Method, Socrates himself is one of them, who argue that the texts do not have to be confined or boxed into printed text. Artifacts, objects, or even physical spaces can also play the role just fine. Indeed, as we have already seen, Socrates himself was very suspicious of the written word. While he clearly acknowledge its usefulness, he was also concerned with the dangers of fixing something into perpetuity as "knowledge." Using texts as part of a Socratic Circle helps to avoid this particular problem.

The Partial elements of an effective Socratic as per Socrates

The Socratic texts are pretty much able to challenge the thinking skills of the participants by embodying the following characteristics:

- Ideas, ideals and values
- The elements of complexity and challenge
- Clear relevance to the curriculum of the participants
- A defined level of ambiguity

When all of these qualities are in place, the text, in a Socratic Method sense, is complete. Let us look at these characteristics closely.

Ideas and Values

With regard to this, the text should be able to introduce values and ideas that in themselves are complex and pose quite the amount of difficulty in their summarization. If all factors are assessed correctly, the most powerful of discussions often arise from connections of the personal kind to ideas that are abstract; from defined implications to personal values.

These kinds of "big picture" questions are precisely what Socrates chose to investigate in his own dialectics. Apart from some of Plato's later dialogues (where Socrates is likely speaking for Plato, rather than for himself), Socrates was almost entirely focused on larger scale, sweeping concerns, such as the nature of truth, knowledge, "the good," and so on. While the Socratic Method can be applied to other topics, it tends to be the most productive when focused on these sorts of grander ideas.

Challenge and Complexity

The text must be rich in complexity. The ideas stacked within the text must be multiple at the very least. Ideally, the text should require multiple readings. Socrates alluded to this on multiple levels. However, the text should neither be too far above the intellectual degree of the participants nor too long in the intellectual degree. Without a proper mixture of complexity on the one hand and accessibility on the other, the text will either fail to elicit an adequate response from students; or, it will fail to engage some of the students for whom it's too difficult to process.

Clear Relevance to the Curriculum of the Participants

A text that is effective in the Socrates sense has indefinable themes but at the same time, they are definable, recognizable to the lives of the participants and pertinent to the same. By all means, all the themes in the text ought to be related to the curriculum of the student body.

A Defined Level of Ambiguity

The text should be approachable, at least from a variety of differing perspectives. This includes perspectives that are observed to be exclusive mutually. The effect here is that critical thinking is stimulated and vital questions, arising from the critical thinking, are raised. Here is the thing- the stark absence of right and wrong replies or answers promote a range of discussion platforms at the same time encouraging individual contributions. Virtually every topic that Socrates ever investigated was highly ambiguous. This absence of right and wrong answers is precisely what the Socratic Method was designed for. Aside from helping the students work through the specific text at hand, using the Socratic Method on such a text will give them valuable tools going forward. Rather than encountering an ambiguous text and feeling stumped, students develop the critical thinking skills necessary to approach the text dialogically and work out their own answers and interpretation.

The Two Different Ways in the Selection of Text

When it comes to Socratic texts, they may be divided into two main categories:

1. Texts in print. This includes poems, short stories as well as essays. Non-print texts such as sculptures, photographs, and maps should be included as well.

2. Subject area. This draws from both non-print and print objects. Language arts may be approached through history and poems, which will then draw from oral or written speeches that are steeped in history.

Chapter 7: Caring For Our Souls

Are you not ashamed that you give your attention to acquiring as much money as possible, and similarly with reputation and honor, and give no attention or thought to truth and understanding and the perfection of your soul? – Socrates

The Socratic concept of the soul is similar to many religious and spiritual beliefs. We tend to accept that there is a part of us which is different from the body and which is considered more important that the body. A good soul is generally considered more desirable than wealth or social reputation. Socrates believed that the goodness of our souls determines whether we live a good life or not.

Socrates believed our souls to be immortal and invisible. He also considered it to be immutable, and permanent. The soul gives life to the body; without it, the body is no longer animated. This is what we experience as death: when the body and soul separate. Perhaps most interesting, though, is the fact that Socrates claimed that the soul *continued to contemplate truth* after it was separated from the body. This meant that the pursuit of the "good life," the pursuit of truth, was not limited just to our time here on earth. Rather, the soul would continue its intellectual pursuits long after the body was gone.

The concept of the 'good life' is very vague. Depending on a person's beliefs, the good life can mean a life of wealth, or good reputation or any of these worldly achievements. For Socrates, of course, 'good life' means a virtuous life.

To highlight this, the term Socrates used in Greek is arête, which literally meant excellence. For example, the areté of a knife is to be sharp because it is used to slice things. For humans, their areté is to be virtuous. Just as the knife is supposed to slice things, humans are supposed to live virtuous lives.

What's interesting to note here is that Socrates is making an enormous assumption. The analogy he presents of the knife is a good one; however, he's glossed over the fact that humans are "supposed to" live virtuous lives. Not only that, but that to live virtuously is our sole purpose in life.

This is interesting for a couple of reasons. First, Socrates has laid out a very specific claim for what human excellence looks like: namely, that excellence is synonymous with virtue. This may seem like a safe claim to make; but, in fact, it makes a lot of assumptions. Even if we agree with Socrates that excellence and virtue are one and the same, one would expect Socrates to scrutinize this idea with the same level of care and detail that he uses to examine other concepts. Surprisingly, though, he doesn't. There's nothing *wrong* with this, per se. But it's an interesting thing to take into account: for all of his focus on "knowing nothing," Socrates is of the very firm and steadfast conviction that human excellence means living virtuously. This goes to show just how important this idea was to Socrates. While virtually everything else he encountered would undergo a massive amount of scrutiny, he's content to accept this equivalence with little fuss.

Second, the claim that our purpose in life is to live virtuously places an enormous amount of importance on the investigation of what a virtuous life actually looks like. After all, if the one thing we're supposed to do in this life is pursue virtue, the same way that a knife is supposed to cut, then what reason is there to waste our time with anything else? This is why Socrates was so incredibly disgusted by the likes of the Sophists, who preferred empty rhetoric and false knowledge to the pursuit of virtue and truth, so long as it meant their enrichment. As we see in the opening quote to this chapter, Socrates believed that the pursuit of personal wealth was pointless, and did nothing to address the importance of living a good, virtuous life, and caring for the soul.

We can have a good soul and thus a good life if we live a virtuous life, and since philosophy encourages us to examine our lives and to constantly do so in case we might be mistaken due to our inherent human fallibility, this is how we ensure we become virtuous. After all, we live according to what we believe in.

In the early Platonic Dialogues, which are generally believed to describe Socrates' ideas, the discussions are usually about what it means to live a virtuous life. For example, what is piety? Is it just to charge one's father of murder because he has neglected the health of a slave? Was Socrates right to accept the Athenian government's sentence of death instead of trying to escape?

The discussions to these questions are too complex, but what we need to point out is the importance of living according to virtue. For example, to answer the last question above, Socrates argued that injustice cannot be an answer to injustice. Even if he was a victim of injustice because he was incorrectly judged as guilty, as a citizen of Athens, he was still required to follow the law. Escaping would mean rejecting Athenian laws and so committing an unjust act.

Though you might disagree with Socrates' view on whether to escape or not, and he would certainly encourage you to think for yourself, the point being made here is that he has thought about it and has come to the conclusion that it is more virtuous not to escape.

With this we see how philosophy, this constant logical examination of one's beliefs, allows one to live a virtuous life. We may make a mistake in our contemplations, and some people may disagree with us, but constant examination is better than none at all.

Socrates was fully convinced that a life of questioning assumptions, pursuing truth, and striving for virtue through an examined life was the only life worth living. He carried these beliefs throughout his entire life, even to the very end.

Chapter 8: The Ethics Of Socrates

Apart from being interested in philosophy, Socrates was interested to a large extent in ethics. He came up with ideologies circling ethics that hold well even today. In this chapter, we bring to you the ethical propaganda of Socrates. Something worth pondering about!

Socrates was in fact considered as the father of ethics as a science! Some of the key attributes of his views towards ethics are as follows:

- Having no big formal education, whatever Socrates learnt later in his life was through the process of self-learning. According to him, every person should resort to self-knowledge as nothing can be more powerful than that.
- Socrates weighed knowledge and virtue equally. In his opinion, man should spend his life pursuing virtue instead of running after material wealth. He also went on to state that virtue can be easily learned just like how knowledge is learned. Contrary to the prevailing belief that one is virtuous by birth, Socrates' statement proposed that virtue can be acquired over one's lifetime. This is an incredibly significant caveat. Given Socrates' belief that pursuit of virtue ought to take precedent above all other pursuits, it's important to note that he did in fact believe virtue can be developed, just like any other skill. Were it not for this, his philosophy would have amounted to a kind of determinism. Fortunately for us, that's not the case!
- There was nothing interesting or lively about a life that is not examined thoroughly. Socrates urged that the pursuit to seek knowledge and wisdom should be the ultimate motivation in people's lives as opposed to their personal interests. He believed that ethical actions stemmed from knowledge and thereby stressed the importance of seeking knowledge.
- Socrates firmly believed that reason was the way to lead a good life. Accordingly, it was believed that true happiness can be achieved by doing the right thing in life. He also stated that when everyone serves their utility, satisfy the needs of their soul, then what is left is true happiness.
- Socrates went on to state that all human actions are driven by some purpose. He dismissed the idea of regarding human behavior as a mechanical activity. According

to him, all human beings strive towards achieving the good through their actions. Their thirst to do the right thing serves as their ultimate purpose in life. This is a strong claim to make: that every human always strives for the good. What Socrates meant, though, was that every human strives to do *what they perceive as good*. Oftentimes, this may not align with what is *actually* good in the world. But, if we assume that Socrates is correct, then this implies that all humans can be led to pursue what is *actually* good, so long as they're educated and led to understand what that looks like. This places an enormous amount of importance on education, and explains why Socrates was so focused on dialogue, the dialectic method, and the pursuit of knowledge. With adequate knowledge, and through the constant examination of one's life, one could uncover the path to living a good, virtuous life. With this in mind, let's discuss the Socratic paradox.

Socratic Paradox:

One of the important contributions of Socrates to the field of ethics was the concept of the Socratic paradox. The Socratic paradox justifies the act of evil by man. The underlying principle on which this theory is based on is that People act immorally but they do not do so deliberately.

Basically, Socrates states that mankind is capable of being immoral and unethical. However, they do not commit such acts deliberately or fully knowing well that their actions are unethical in nature.

The key attributes of the Socratic paradox are as follows:

- People tend to seek things that are beneficial for their interests. They pursue only those things that would benefit them and their interests. Man is not interested in pursuing things that are against his own interests.
- According to Socrates, man is aware of what is good and right, his actions will be directed only towards achieving it.
- If a person commits an immoral act, it is because he did not know that it was immoral to begin with. Had he known the right way to achieve his purpose, he would have resorted to that course of action only.

- If man possessed adequate amount of knowledge, he would be able to seek the right things that would be beneficial for his interests.
- Nobody is capable of harming themselves. So, if anybody is harmed, it is because the person acted without the knowledge of the harm and is not to be blamed.
- Based on this, man's knowledge or lack of knowledge was responsible for his happiness.
- Everybody strives to seek the good. If they fail to do so, it is either because of their lack of knowledge as to how to seek it or their ignorance.

If you look at it, the Socratic paradox judges the good nature of a person's soul based on the amount of the knowledge possessed by that person. If a person was knowledgeable, he was always righteous as he would be able to seek the good at all times with the knowledge he possessed. On the other hand, a person was considered evil when he did not possess the sufficient knowledge to seek the good.

There are several criticisms stacked up against the Socratic paradox. Some of the prominent ones are as follows:

- According to the concept of Socratic paradox, a person was capable of immoral acts only when he is not aware that it is immoral to begin with. It portrays evil as an involuntary act and there is no underlying motive. However, if evil was indeed an involuntary action, then it is not possible to hold any one guilty for that particular action.
- The concept suggests that people will seek the good if they have knowledge about how to seek it as it would help them achieve their real interests. However, that is not the case in reality. People do not seek the good at all times even if they have knowledge about it.
- Socrates suggests that morality flows from knowledge. People resort to immoral ways only due to the lack of knowledge. If this principle was indeed true, then it should be possible to resolve the issues that arise out of immorality with the help of knowledge. However, that is not the practical solution to all solutions involving moral values.
- According to the Socratic paradox, people would not resort to evil if they knew beforehand that the specific action was evil in nature. However, Aristotle criticized this saying that it is entirely possible for man to resort to immoral activities fully

aware that he is committing an act of evil. Despite knowing the right way to do things, mankind may still resort to choose the wrong path.

Apart from the above, the term Socratic paradox also refers to Socrates' famous quote – "I know that I know nothing". As mentioned earlier, Socrates never claimed to have known things or claimed to be wise. He was well aware of his ignorance unlike the many people belonging to the noble family in those days.

Socrates laid the foundation of what we have known today as the science of ethics. Even though his assumptions about the ethical nature of human beings were contested and criticized by many, it set the stage for the future to build on this.

Indeed, Aristotle's *Nichomachean Ethics*, perhaps the most foundational work on ethical philosophy in the Western tradition, was made possible thanks to Socrates' innovations. While Aristotle, student of Plato, criticizes Socrates for his paradoxical position, he is still indebted to Socrates for pioneering a path into ethical inquiry in the first place. Before Socrates, philosophers were almost wholly concerned with natural phenomena. Thanks to his focus on living "the good life" and pursuing a virtuous existence, philosophy came to include a significant amount of inquiry into the nature of values and the pursuit of an ethical life. Much of western philosophy since Socrates has concerned itself with how to live morally. We have him to thank for this philosophical turn.

Chapter 9: Trial and Death Of Socrates

Before we deal with the trial of Socrates, it is necessary that we understand the series of events that triggered Socrates being charged in the first place. As we have already discussed, Athens was the embodiment of democracy even in those days. Every citizen had enough freedom to do things at his will and all the male citizens of the city were members of the Assembly.

When Athens lost to Sparta in the Peloponnesian war, the Pandora's Box was kicked open. Even though the Athenians enjoyed complete freedom under the democratic regime in Athens, the entire population was not satisfied with just that. On the other hand, there was Sparta with its aristocratic set up where in the elite group of people decided what was best for the state.

Education boomed under the Spartan rule more so than it ever did in Athens. Even though Sparta was their arch enemy, most of the Athenian youth admired Sparta and the Spartans. The fact that they had suffered a terrible defeat in the hands of Sparta did not deter them from admiring Sparta.

It was at this point when the Athenian government started growing restless at the growing number of the fans of Sparta. No system will succeed and withstand when all the people in the system do not believe in it. This was precisely what happened with the perfectly happy go lucky democratic system prevalent in Athens. There were several youth who protested against the State and sought to bring the democracy down.

Trial

As mentioned earlier, Socrates was not a big fan of the democracy that was prevailing in Athens. He was the biggest critic of the Athenian democracy. Naturally, many of his followers shared his distaste towards democracy. Socrates took up the role of the moral critic of the society and went on to question the moral values propagated by the State.

The tensions caused by such open expressions of distaste against the government increased substantially after the war with the Spartans came to an end. Several religious scandals, which were initiated by many followers of Socrates and the attempts to overthrow the democratic rule, were the tipping points for the Athenian Government. It was no surprise when the Athenian government decided to charge Socrates with impiety.

When Socrates was brought to trial, his reputation for stirring trouble against the government and his open proclamations of displeasure with the government in the past acted against him. Along with the charges of impiety, Socrates was also held responsible for polluting the minds of Athenian youth and driving them to commit crimes against the Athenian government.

Proceedings:

As was the usual practice, once a person was convicted, they were brought to trial followed by a formal accusation. The jury for the trial was selected by drawing lots of the names of the male volunteers who wished to be the jurors for the trial. During the trial, three people spoke against Socrates accusing him of the charges under which he was convicted. His association with Critias and Alcibiades, who were responsible for many protests against the Athenian government, was one of the important reasons why Socrates was dragged into a trial in the first place.

Plato and Xenophon's accounts of the trial are the only sources of Socrates' speech during the trial. Even though there were stark differences in both the accounts, there were enough common elements in their accounts to give us a sufficent overview of the trial.

Socrates was accused of not acknowledging the gods of Athens and for introducing other deities. Socrates' defense spoke about his utmost devotion to the gods. However his defense was too complicated for not just the jury to comprehend but also for the other citizens of Athens.

Socrates mentioned about a divine voice that served as his guide and was responsible for giving him constant advice since his childhood. Why was this thought bizarre for the Athenians to assimilate? In fact, Meletus, who was the main accuser in the case, mocked Socrates for basing his judgment on an imaginary voice.

The Athenians had never heard of a mortal being guided by a divine voice. The closest thing they could relate to was the concept of a seer who was in touch with the divine and could predict the future. As was the custom then, seers were appointed by the Athenian government to offer their religious services to the State. However, Socrates was not appointed to any such office. He was therefore not abiding by the general procedure and policy adopted by the State and was influencing people with his divine intervention.

It was based on that voice that Socrates based his relationships with the others. His involvement in the public affairs was also based on the guidance he received from this voice. Hence the whole concept of piety suggested and practiced by Socrates was not only unorthodox but also impossible for the jurors to comprehend that the gods would want such chaos in the first place through a mortal like Socrates.

Even though there were many suggestions about his decision to stay and face the trial, Plato's account explicitly states in his account that Socrates had decided to go through the trial and answer all the questions honestly, solely because it was the path suggested by the divine voice guiding him, even though such a course of action had the possibility of being fatal to Socrates.

Leading up to his trial, Socrates was already considered a moral and intellectual nuisance in Athens. Aristophanes, a playwright who was one of his contemporaries, even went so far as to depict Socrates as a Sophist in one of his plays--something that must have been intensely frustrating for Socrates, who despised the Sophists. Many ancient Athenians, however, believed that Socrates has imbued the youth with a nihilistic and dismissive attitude toward tradition, the same as the Sophists.

During his defense, Socrates claimed that he had "attached himself" to the city, much as a gadfly stings a horse to rouse it to awareness. He also argued that he was a god's gift to the city of Athens, to help its citizens increase their knowledge and virtuous capacity. Further, Socrates was widely known for claiming that democracy, or the opinion of the majority, was not the correct way to approach the governance of a state. Rather, proper policy stems from possessing the right knowledge and competency, things that are possessed by just a handful of the populace. This would imply Socrates' support of something akin to oligarchy; and, given his reputed relationship with various oligarchic figures, it's far from unlikely that Socrates would have openly supported such a system in opposition to the reigning Athenian democratic government. Indeed, Socrates is reportedly recorded as having supported the openly autocratic Spartan government.

Socrates appeared before a jury of what was, based on our historical knowledge, likely comprised of at least 500 Athenian men. According to Plato's account, the vote was almost equally divided: if just a few dozen men had changed their vote, Socrates may indeed have been acquitted. One wonders how different the legacy of western philosophy would be were Socrates to have survived.

After being sentenced to death, Socrates' supporters begged him to flee the city. This was, by all accounts, something that even his accusers expected him to do. It's fairly clear, in fact, that no one involved in Socrates' trial actually expected him to suffer the death penalty. Even those who despised him were primarily focused on simply *getting him to leave Athens*. There's not much evidence that anyone actually wished for Socrates' death.

Nevertheless, he opted for death because he believed, on principle, that adherence to the law of Athens was of maximum importance. Socrates was, without a doubt, a man of principle--until the very end.

Chapter 10: Socrates' Legacy

Alexander the Great

Alexander the Great is undoubtedly one of the most heralded military leaders ever. His conquests saw the expansion of Greece to encompass modern day Greece, Macedonia, Bulgaria, nearly the entire Middle-East, and parts of Africa. He was one of the first people from the Mediterranean world to explore into the Indian subcontinent and conquered part of what he explored. At this time, his kingdom was the largest in the known world.

Not only was he a military commander but he also brought forth the enlightenment of the Hellenistic civilization. He was the Andrew Carnegie of his time building libraries across the known world, including the ever important Library of Alexandria. His conquests brought knowledge from all parts of the known world and took the Greek language with him. This was quite possibly the first show of a lingua franca (working language) and an impressive show of international trade.

Trade took place from country to country, along the Mediterranean and through Europe, Africa and Asia. Wine was traded from one country for spices from another. Linen was traded for copper. The Mediterranean world was connected.

The line of direct tutelage appears to have stopped with Alexander as he was entirely too busy governing the needs of an entire country, one that was expanding at that, to take up any sole students. His life, image, and ability were admired for centuries after though and were a prominent part of Roman history. The great Roman commanders, politicians and emperors used Alexander as an image to strive for.

His abilities won him the renown of a man that reached godly ability so he was even that much more sought over. Until Alexander, people would strive to achieve what the gods could or to model their lives like the demi-gods of Greek mythology but Alexander gave them a flesh and blood example of absolute greatness. Just like Alexander's conquest of the known world of his time, the reach of Rome spread far and wide to every area it could.

Alexander was one of Aristotle's premier pupils. Without the philosophical knowledge that passed from Socrates, to Plato, to Aristotle, and finally to Alexander, his conquest may have taken a very different shape. He carried with him a sense of intellectual duty, not unlike the one purported by Socrates himself.

Aristotle

If Alexander the Great was the embodiment of physical power and strategy, Aristotle is undoubtedly then the embodiment of the mind and mental prowess. By trade Aristotle was a teacher and a philosopher. Now his study of philosophy is not what we would understand it as because at that time philosophy encompassed nearly all areas of thought including science, math, logic, rhetoric, and so on. Essentially philosophy was anything and everything that dealt with discovery and higher learning. So this age of history wasn't really as "philosophic" as we'd consider but it did have quite a few bright minds that would make great discoveries.

Among the areas that Aristotle shown light on was nature, logic, moderation, and more. He was the person to first identify plants and animals as living creatures. He also provided reasoning to why there is a difference between plants, animals and humans. He provided that the first two have souls and animals have the power of mobility in addition to this but only humans had intellect. This was the first concept on plants and animals of the time.

Aristotle then went on to shape logic through systematic reasoning. He used inference and deduction to break apart arguments to determine whether they were right or wrong. This was an area his two predecessors had a lot of direct influence over but Aristotle was able to shape this into a system. Logic is still used today in nearly the same way he taught it to his pupils in Ancient Greece. Students are still taught logic and rhetoric as a fundamental tool for reasoning.

Indeed, Aristotle is considered by most contemporary philosophers to be the father of modern logic. Without Aristotle's contributions, our current approach to logic and reasoning would look dramatically different. Aristotle's focus on syllogism, propositions, conclusions, formal logic, and especially his work on logical fallacies came to shape the entire future of western philosophy for centuries.

The idea of moderation was unheard of prior to Aristotle's time as well. The social hierarchy had everything and the lower rungs of the social ladder had close to nothing. Life was either spent in excess or in extreme abstinence. Aristotle's Golden Mean taught that there was an ideal median between greed and frugal living. His forerunners did have influence in this area but Aristotle took it to new limits and wrote it down. He also expounds a lot on the difference between direct action and inaction.

Aristotle was a firm opponent of the Spartan role because it only focused on one thing and never on the median. This was once again another direct influence from his fore-teachers who also not only spoke against Spartan role but also taught this concept of the Golden Mean, once again Aristotle was able to systemize it.

Plato

"A man must understand to choose the mean and be wary of extremes," – Socrates

Plato was the direct student of Socrates and pays homage to him in every chance he gets. Plato is most famous for two books that he wrote, The Republic and The Symposium, in which he prominently features Socrates. Socrates philosophy was heavily focused on ideas of logical arguments, love, politics, and ability, in knowledge at least.

The famous dialogues of Plato personify his ideas through discussion between several people in which they break down ideas in a logical manner. This is undoubtedly something he inherited from his teach Socrates because in his book The Republic, he uses the character of Socrates to break down the ideas of Plato's brother's character. Ideas are brought forth in a very immature state and through this systematic and logical review, the ideas are refined to something more scientific and credible.

The root of the word "Platonic" from the phrase "Platonic love" comes from comes from Plato's namesake. This was a theory of his that showed there are several ways to love another which was a huge step for the then lust-infested Greek culture. His idea was you could love a child because they are your child but this love was separated from any sort of fleshly context. Additionally, this type of love could be exercised in several different ways apart from just that of your child and also applied to friends, family and other acquaintances regardless of age.

Politics was another theme that was heavily subscribed to in Plato's theories. Once again, in The Republic Plato uses characters to discuss different types of political structures. He discusses Tyranny, Democracy, Oligarchy, Timocracy, and Aristocracy as the 5 types of political systems discussed in The Republic with Aristocracy being the ideal system of governance. An Aristocracy is a system of government that is ruled over by the philosophic elite (the learned class), with two additional classes to support them – the protectors of the ruling class and the working class that made up the majority. If Aristocracy is mismanaged, it would result in Timocracy which is led by people more suited for military leadership. Again, the breakdown of Timocracy leads to an Oligarchy which is the rich dictating to the poor. After an Oligarchy comes a Democracy where everyone governs themselves (slightly different than modern day Democracy), which Plato feels is unsuitable because of the lack of knowledge that the poor have and resembles more Anarchy since everyone does what they want. Finally, Democracy unfolds in Tyranny which is a state of chaos where power is seized by one person that is capable of doing so and is then hated by the people he rules.

A better understanding of his political views comes from his idea of how people are born. Plato believed that people are not clean-slates at birth and that they already have some sort of inclination towards their future development. The smart are born smart, the strong are born strong and the peasant is born a peasant. This is why he used his narrative on governance to explain why everyone couldn't rule because not everyone was born too. Unintelligent people were not fit in his mind to govern others.

This is not far removed from Socrates' own beliefs regarding democracy, as discussed earlier. Socrates felt that rule by the masses (in the form of democracy) was bound to lead to ruin, whereas the capable few could lead the popular form through an oligarchic or aristocratic form of government. It's fairly clear, then, where Plato's idea of perfect governance stem from.

The life of Plato is worth a deeper look because he was the direct student of Socrates and most of what is known about Socrates actually comes from the narratives of Plato. The Republic is thought to be the view of not only Plato but his teacher as well. Most of Plato's views actually come directly from the teaching of Socrates. Although he had a mix of other teachers as well, Socrates was by far the most influential. Understanding Plato more, then gives a better idea of how to understand Socrates.

Chapter 11: Socrates' Contribution to Modern Human Civilization

I have a firm hope that there is something in store for those who have died, and as we have been told for many years, something much better for the good than for the wicked.
– Socrates

The idea of living a virtuous life is not limited to the ancient Greeks. Ancient civilizations like the Egyptians have already accepted the idea of an afterlife, and that those who lived good lives would be rewarded while those who lived bad lives would be punished. What made the ancient Greeks different, particularly the Athenians, was that they rejected the absolute authority of priests or kings on matters regarding morality. Though philosophers existed, the good ones like Socrates still encouraged their followers to think for themselves.

This is precisely what Socrates' life's work focused on: the idea that each individual must pursue for themselves what is moral, virtuous, and good. Given his belief in the immortality of the soul, it's clear that Socrates was strongly in favor of the individual perfection of the soul throughout our mortal lives. Socrates focused a great deal of his energy on encouraging his fellow Athenians to pursue excellence--that is, a virtuous life--while they had the chance.

It is thought that this would never have happened if Athens did not follow democracy. Due to this unique form of government, men were able to think freely for themselves. Knowledge did not become a monopoly, a luxury for the few. Of course some people would argue that knowledge was still a monopoly because it was only for male citizens, but it is important to understand that women in the ancient world were considered inferior compared to men.

This is an interesting argument, though, considering Socrates' own distaste for democratic government. On the one hand, democracy seems to have lent a hand to Socrates' own capacity to pursue truth, knowledge, and virtue. On the other, Socrates is clearly critical of the destructive potential of democracy in the hands of mob rule.

The Socratic understanding of philosophy can deepen a person's faith by providing a logical basis for the virtues taught by religion. Religion can sometimes turn people off because of some religious leaders' insistence that everything must be accepted as based on God's absolute law. By showing that the lessons provided by religion regarding a virtuous life can be logically debated upon, people may find new understand in God's word.

Furthermore, with Socrates' lessons in mind, we can understand that a person can be virtuous even without believing in a religion. Many people make the mistake that those who do not believe in God, e.g. the atheists, agnostics and non-religious people, cannot live a "good life". They can, in fact, be virtuous by studying themselves through the theories of philosophy.

Legacy: How Have Other Philosophers Understood Socrates?

Over the centuries, the majority of philosophy schools have had positive things to say about Socrates, with many being influenced by him in regards to their own notions. Socrates' works have been featured in many other works, from the classical period to contemporary philosophy. Many schools and disciplines within the realm of philosophy, in fact, owe their existence to the pioneering nature of Socrates' work. The ancient Greeks and Romans, as well as modern and contemporary western philosophers, would not be where they are without the efforts of Socrates.

Hellenistic Philosophy

The Cynics

Socrates was greatly respected by the cynics and their own philosophies originate with him. Diogenes of Sinope was one of the earliest Cynic and whilst no genuine works of his has survived (the majority of our evidence comes from circumstantial sources), scholars have credited him with various works. Diogenes of Sinope attempted to challenge standard customs as a base for ethical values and substitute it with character. He describe that happiness was a combination of liberty and self-determination and would be available to anyone who exercised their bodies and thoughts.

The word cynic, in fact, derives from an ancient Greek word meaning "dog." The Cynics were sometimes called the "dog philosophers," because of their living habits. They chose to live on the streets, with no concern for their standard of living, and completely dissociated from the norms of everyday Greek society. This is not unlike Socrates, who argued that focusing on personal wealth and status was meaningless when compared to the importance of excellence, virtue, knowledge, and the good life.

The Cynics were, also like Socrates, cast out by their contemporaries from normal social circles. Their philosophy was colored by this treatment, and it's no surprise that they identified with Socrates, a venerable ancient philosopher who had been treated similarly.

The Stoics

The Stoics were another philosophy school who greatly admired Socrates. The founder of the Stoics was a man named Zeno who became interested in philosophy after learning about Socrates and his beliefs. The Stoics considered themselves as genuine Socratic believers, particularly when it came to the notion of absolute control of ethical virtuousness to ethical superiority, the thought of ethical superiority as a form of wisdom and the requirement of this in order to attain true happiness.

Zeno is recognized for his depiction of being good as a 'smooth flow of life' and it was this, in part, that made the concept of elenchus (a logical refutation; an argument that refutes another argument by proving the contrary of its conclusion) since it could highlight contradictions in the thoughts and deeds of other people, which could interrupt lives. When one did not hold justification for an action or thought, your life would not flow smoothly. However, if you could hold your reason up to analysis then it would be rational and constant. Therefore, the elenchus was a significant test and the Stoics believed that anyone who could endure it was knowledgeable, whereas anyone who couldn't were claimed to be unknowing.

Socrates philosophy was also used within Roman Stoicism, especially by Seneca and Epictetus, who respected his strong personality. Seneca particularly praises him for his steadfast consistency to his beliefs even when he faced considerable obstacles and how he looked to care for his soul.

The elenchus was one aspect of Socrates that Epictetus was greatly interested in. His comprehension of the method is somewhat different to that of Socrates': Epictetus tells that it is important to realize that we are all ignorant to what is necessary. He would inspire his supporters to exercise this test on themselves, stating that it was a method Socrates himself practiced, since living an examined life was important.

The Skeptics

The Skeptics roughly believed that we should be apprehensive or reserve judgment of total assertions of certainty or knowledge. To many Skeptics, especially Pyrrhonian skeptics, Socrates was seen as an extremist but then occasionally he was seen as a Skeptic.

Arcesilaus, the initial head of the Skeptic school, used Socrates' method of using ignorance to test the answers his students would give and then counter them. Cicero himself stated that Socrates was recognized as sanctioning the contention that no one can know anything apart from his or her own ignorance.

The Skeptics were a curious philosophical school. One of their leaders actually claimed, at one point, to be afraid to take a step, for fear that his belief that the ground was there might actually be false. This can be interpreted as an incredibly intense and extreme version of Socrates' position that he "knows that he knows nothing." In fact, the Skeptic philosophy as a whole is attributable to Socratic roots in this way.

The Epicurean

Whilst the majority of schools admired and respected Socrates' beliefs, the Epicureans were one of a few that disapproved of him. Some scholars believe this was partly due to their attitude towards the Stoics who did respect him. For the Epicureans, Socrates was described as an obscurantist and a skeptic who disregarded the natural world in order to focus on ethical questions that resulted in no resolutions. Colotes condemns Socrates speech within the *Phaedrus* that he doesn't know anything and Philodemus says that integrity can't be learned.

A number of works were produced by the Epicureans who criticized him, which included the *Gorgias* and the *Euthydemus*. Within the former, Socrates is mistrustful of the idea that pleasure is inherently valuable and his perseverance that pleasure is not the complement of the virtuous. Pleasure was stated to be liberty from disturbance, or *ataraxia*, and this was good for the human soul. Socrates criticizes Callicles for embracing hedonism, a lifestyle that was opposite to his own beliefs, and Epicurus openly states that they are not in favor of profligacy. However, the Epicureans did associate pleasure as a positive thing and the notion that pleasure is something negative did not commend Socrates to them.

That said, though, Socrates seemed more in favor of what his student's student (Plato's student, Aristotle) actually argued for: namely, the idea of the Golden Mean. To call Socrates a skeptic or an absolute poverty focused minimalist would be unfair. He favored a balanced life: one which took into consideration immediate needs, but which also focused on the all-important pursuit of virtue, knowledge, and the good life. The Epicurean criticism of him, then, is almost certainly fundamentally flawed.

Another reason why the Epicureans did not admire Socrates was how he used irony. Cicero claims that Epicurus found Socrates' method of presenting himself as foolish yet still praising others such as Gorgias and Protagoras somewhat disgraceful. For the Epicureans, if Socrates wished to say something, then he should say it.

The Peripatetics

The Peripatetics were the students of Aristotle and either refused to say anything about him or attacked him ferociously. To the Peripatetics, Socrates was an adulterer, an allegation which caused such a commotion that Panatius, a Stoic, had to produce a repudiation of it. For the Peripatetics, Socrates concentration to ethics was undesirable in philosophy.

Modern Philosophy

Hegel

Hegel referred to Socrates as "the great historic turning point", claiming that two contrasting positives came into impact. These were one's consciousness and the universal law. Before Socrates, ethics and morals existed but they were not Socratic. Namely, that goodness was everywhere but did not have the principle of one's consciousness. Morals existed unconditionally, guiding everyone's lives without them contemplating on it. Universal law possesses the decree of the gods and therefore had a universal authority that was understood by everyone.

For Hegel, Socrates was the first to understand and recognize a change in the affiliation between a person and morals. The present has to justify the consciousness. Hegel credits Socrates with the method of presenting questions regarding what we should do as well as the acts that the government has set. With Socrates, the consciousness has shifted and now the law should answer to the consciousness. Hegel claims that Socrates' way of asking questions allows individuals to break away from unexamined compliance and instead lets them question ethical values as a state. This was a moment of unique historical progress in the world of philosophy and intellectualism, and something that Hegel forcefully praised.

Hegel basically discovers Socrates had skepticism towards everyday acceptance which leaves behind an uncertain knowledge and that the consciousness needs to be able to examine and reflect. Although Hegel ascribes the same skepticism to the sophists, he gives Socrates far more credit and respect. Because of Socrates, consciousness of the world around us and within us is greater. Asking what is nature leads to asking what is truth and the affiliation between self-consciousness and reality develops into the principal philosophy matter.

Kierkegaard

Kierkegaard claims that Socrates is not as virtuous and ethical as philosophical history has presented him but instead, he is an ironist. Not only is he an ironist in what he says and does, but he himself is full of irony. Aristophanes presents Socrates in quite an overstated and embellished way and Kierkegaard states that this representation was close to what Socrates was like. He disputes Hegel's view that Socrates ushered in a new era in philosophy and maintains the restrictions of Socrates irony demonstrates to the requirement for religion. Kierkegaard also states that Socrates use of irony was a means of beginning the advancement of self-consciousness and that this was all Socrates could offer.

Late in his career, Kierkegaard states that he believes he has overlooked Socrates importance in regards to religion and ethics. Within his *My Task*, Kierkegaard says that it his task to reinvigorate Christianity and sees himself as a modern day, Christian Socrates in that he tries to stimulate Christians from their everyday contentment into being aware that their religion allows them to convey their personal partiality. Kierkegaard's request is comparable to Socrates' call to acknowledge your own ignorance in that he is not really a Christian although he is more than his own generation.

Nietzsche

Nietzsche is well known for his vicious attacks on Socrates in his *The Birth of Tragedy*. He claims that it was Socrates and logical thinking that gave rise to an era of decadence in Athens. The fragile balance between order and restraint with revelry and indulgence was first found in the plays of Aeschylus that allowed Euripides' rationalism to develop. Euripides was considered to be a guise for Socrates and the Greeks were corrupted by aesthetic Socratism – where the audience had to unravel the meaning in the sorrow of the characters instead of just soaking in the emotions.

Nietzsche then attacks Socrates in later works. Socrates is a representation of the lower classes and using irony shows him as an embellishment as well as a disguise. Because he is lower class, he has no other way of communicating and used his questions in order to conquer his opponents.

Nietzsche went so far as to argue that all of Socrates' purported ignorance, his claim that he only "knew that he knew nothing," was completely contrived. In Nietzsche's mind, Socrates was faking it all along. He felt that Socrates was using this position as a way to plead ignorance, simply with the aim of eliciting a response from his interlocutor that he could then use to attack, pin, and take advantage of the other person. For Nietzsche, Socrates was the ultimate Sophist: he pretended to offer wisdom, but actually only sought to advance his own standing.

However, we can clearly see that Nietzsche still had quite a large amount of respect for Socrates, even though it was hesitant. He tells that Socrates was a great influence and praised that he held onto his virtues – and his virtues continued after his death – due to the way in which he was executed.

Heidegger

Heidegger had a close relationship with Socrates in that they both believed that truth was due to looking at things in a particular way. He credits Socrates with that it is the progression of inquiry that leads to the truth. Socrates was able to produce the negative and ultimately the truth – the converser's explanation - through the process of questions. As such, Socrates was not concerned in conveying the suggestions regarding virtue or truth but instead was focused on continuing to ask questions relating to it, which maintains its intricate uniformity. Piety, or virtue, cannot be spoken but numerous acts of pious deeds leads to piety and through quiet examination of those deeds will it reveal itself.

It is in this quietness that Heidegger is different from the ancient philosopher. Socrates focused on asking questions to others, whereas Heidegger focuses on being open to truth without the requirement of verbal communication with others.

Gadamer

Gadamer was a student of Heidegger and also believed that truth and method was essential in philosophy. However, his science of interpretation led him to maintain that opposition as dialog was important. Gadamer states that whereas philosophical dialogue offers complete truth since it surpasses all its limited suggestions, the science of interpretation also has the duty of illuminating the total truth in all its relationships. What makes Gadamer different to others is that he states we are already within an open dialogue at all times. Conversing with others is not a distraction; it is just another facet of truth. Gadamer says that this is why Plato would only communicate his philosophical beliefs in conversation – that it was both a tribute to Socrates and a manifestation of his belief that both the world and the Individual would find conformity in others.

Gadamer also believed that Socrates' conversations were important not because by living an unexamined life we do not know what is ethical, but we ourselves won't be ethical unless we ask questions just like Socrates.

Five Ways to Live an Examined Life

Socrates has inspired countless throughout the centuries, from politicians to world leaders, from businessmen to farmers. Even today, his belief on living an examined life has inspired others to do the same.

It's easy to understand why. There's something fundamentally stirring and appealing about Socrates' claim that we all ought to live an examined life, in order for our lives to have any worth. That may, in fact, be the reason that you've opted to take on the task of reading this book!

How, then, do we live an examined life? This idea seems too simple in the words of Socrates. But, today, in our complex, modern world, how do we actually pursue this ideal?

Clarify the Why

Why we do or say something may sound so simple initially, or even trifling, but it is important to understand the root cause of making the decisions that we do on a daily basis. As we live our lives we need to proceed consciously, clarifying our reasons why we are striving for a particular career, starting a family with someone, whether we take certain risks, moving to a new location or even not doing anything. Ask yourself questions: is it fear that stops me? Am I certain this is what I want to do? And, am I doing this for me or because society tells me to?

When it comes to all the big decisions you face in life – marriage, kids, career change, study, moving etc. – you should always ask yourself why. Clarifying the why may halt you in your tracks for a bit but it is better to stop for a moment to determine that you are going the way you want, or need, then finding yourself somewhere you really don't want to be.

Looking at Plato's earliest dialogues, where Socrates is probably depicted most accurately, we constantly see him attempting to clarify the why with his interlocutors. Time and time again, he encounters other Athenians who hold firm, steadfast positions, but who have an incredible amount of trouble attempting to elucidate *why* they believe the things that they do. This is often Socrates' first foothold on the path to shaking them loose from erroneous beliefs.

Determine Your Currency

Determining your currency doesn't mean discovering what it is you will pay for in life, but rather what will get you through life. For some people, that means they won't use their beauty to get where they want, instead they will use their brains and by hard work. Determining your currency is an individual realization, and will only be clarified when we are truly honest with ourselves and accept of who we are.

Many of us go through putting ourselves down – we are too fat, too skinny, not smart enough, not beautiful enough – and by doing so, we reduce our worth. When we find out what it is that makes us unique, we can then highlight these gifts. If you are uncertain as to what your gifts are, then ask someone you love what your biggest strengths are and if there is anything they believe could be holding you back. There are times in our lives when we cannot see who we truly are and we can only see ourselves when others tell us what they see.

Practice Self-Control

It is only when we have determined what it is that drives us to make our decisions and what our currency in life is, that we can then learn and apply self-discipline. This doesn't mean that you have to deny yourself of all you want; instead, it means that you think about what it is that you really want and deny yourself the unimportant things.

Socrates, Plato, and Aristotle all focused extensively on the importance of temperance, or placing limitations on our wants. For Socrates, the virtuous life explicitly forbid the pursuit of excess, extravagance, personal wealth, and the like. A life in pursuit of the good, or a life focused on excellence, necessarily included a focus on self-control.

Recognize How Much Control Money Has

It has often been thought that to be happy you need to have money, that more of one will increase the other. However, it is not money, which makes us happy, but what we are able to do with it that makes is happy. This could mean saving up to put a deposit down on a new house, paying for a once in a lifetime experience, saving for a child's education etc. – instead of purchasing wasteful items. The way you use your money is just the same way as you use your brain and your gifts – if used wisely then it is good.

Remember that Socrates firmly believed that pursuit of the good was an innate human quality. Humans would only pursue what they thought to be good. This may or may not be what is *actually* good, depending on the level of knowledge of an individual person. In Socrates' time, the Sophists pursued personal wealth while peddling false, rhetorical knowledge for the sake of profit. This pursuit of profit for profit's sake was abhorrent to Socrates. Instead, he encouraged people to pursue their own personal development, with the ultimate aim of living a just and virtuous life.

Define What is Really Just

There is an old saying – "*Power tends to corrupt, and absolute power corrupts absolutely*". These, and other truthful statements, are the same when it comes to living an examined life. It is necessary to fully recognize the reason for the laws set upon us by the state or society, as well as any unspoken rules, prior to standing up and proclaiming that they are unfair or that their logic is illogical. Even Martin Luther King Junior stated it was one's moral duty to challenge unjust laws. The solution is to look and examine before acting with self-discipline and control if the laws are justified or to stand up against them if they are not just so that just laws can be put into place.

Conclusion

When we live an examined life, just as Socrates suggested thousands of years ago, we find that we benefit greatly.

Top Ten Philosophies of Socrates Which Have Taught Us

After 2,500 years, the philosophies of Socrates have stayed with us even if the man himself is lost to us in time. His beliefs and concepts of human nature, piety, justice and many others are still applicable today as it was back in ancient Athens.

In these top ten philosophies of Socrates, we will look at some of the greatest notions given to us, which have stood the test of time and are still relevant.

They Have Never Been Outdated

Unlike that of many other intellectual disciplines from antiquity, Socrates' philosophies are just as relevant today as they were back in 5th century BCE Athens, or when Plato wrote them. Indeed, it was Socrates' philosophies, which influenced numerous other intellectual schools throughout history, even in contemporary Western philosophy. Basically, all philosophy schools have been constructed on the concepts presented by Socrates and his students. Socrates' focus on ethics, epistemology, and the pursuit of truth contributed to the growth of western philosophy. Rather than continuing to focus on semi-mythological explanations for the world, Socrates gave birth to a philosophical tradition centered on how we ought to live our lives.

He Showed Us How Important It is to Question Everything

Socrates once said, "*The highest form of human excellence is to question oneself and others*". This system of questioning – by conversing with one or a few people with an opposite opinion to yours and questioning the statements, with both sides seeking the absolute truth – showed us how important it is to question everything we hear, say or do. Even today, this process is used in philosophy, the arts and even science, starting with a theory and then breaking it down until you have come to an absolute conclusion.

Prior to Socrates, it was commonplace to accept the existing wisdom handed down to your from your elders and other teachers. Socrates shook this tradition to its foundation, arguing instead that it is our job to question all of the things we take for granted in our day to day lives. This spirit has lived on for centuries, encouraging innovation in both the humanities and the sciences.

We Learned That Life is Insignificant Without Happiness

Through understanding our actions and direction in life, working our way towards happiness (his term for well-being and not the modern-day equivalent of the word) then we are not living our lives. Yes, we may continue going to work, pay the bills etc., but is that really living? Socrates taught us that we need to stop and reflect, becoming aware of the world around us and create a mindful connection with our lives. Socrates asked whether battleships and defensive walls were really needed unless the people they were designed to protect were happy. This is just as true now as it was back in ancient Athens. If we are not aware of our well-being, our happiness, why do we continue slogging away?

Recall that Socrates equated happiness with the pursuit of our ultimate human purpose; which, for him, was to live a virtuous life. Socrates, then, is reminding us that we must constantly pursue what is virtuous if we are to live fulfilling, meaningful lives.

We Learned to Question if Any War is Just

Socrates, as mentioned earlier, states that it is better to suffer an injustice than to commit one. Socrates, although well known as the great father of western philosophy, was a seasoned military man who fought within the Peloponnesian War. He saw great bloodshed, an infinite amount of pain, and was the only one to stand up against the illegal motion to convict the generals as a sole group for abandoning the bodies of the Athenian dead at the sea-battle at Arginusae in 406 BCE. When the Athenians were defeated in the

Peloponnesian War in 404 BCE, Socrates blatantly ignored the command by the Thirty Tyrants to arrest a man who was innocent. As a result, Socrates was one of the first men in ancient Greece to ask the question: is there really a just war? Can war justify the death and pain of thousands? In today's world – with several wars and battles going on – it is still an incredibly relevant question to ask.

Socrates Encouraged True Freedom of Speech

Athens was one of the foremost governments, which allowed people, all people, and the freedom to say what they wanted. Everyone, whether you were a farmer to a wealthy merchant, could speak at the Athenian Assembly, even if they had to do so knowing their place. It was Socrates who rebelled against this tradition through the development of free speech through dialogues. Even though Athens was not keen on this, Socrates carried on speaking as he saw fit even when he paid for it with his life. He was one of the earliest figures to promote the notion of being able to speak your mind without fear – something that is a central part of many governments and nations today. Ironically, in spite of the fact that Socrates was himself a critic of democratic government, he exercised what we would now acknowledge to be a democratic right. His exercise of this right is precisely what allowed him to contribute to Athenian society, and secured him a permanent place in the history of western philosophy.

Socrates Developed Philosophical Ethics

Socrates would ask many questions such as "how do you live the right way?". There were only a handful of philosophers in the ancient world to encourage not only their followers, but scholars and common people, to focus on what is right and wrong instead of concerning themselves with the natural world. By doing so, Socrates developed philosophical ethics – the deliberation as to what is good and evil – which has gone on to help create many ethical and legal policies throughout the history of Western civilizations.

Socrates Was a Supporter of Human Virtues

Socrates may have started life as a poor man but it was his time in the army and witnessing so much bloodshed and war that helped developed his concept of human virtue against *lex talionis*, or the concept of an eye for an eye mentality. The battles he had been involved in over the years had led him to wanting something peaceful, something decent.

Through self-control, discipline, piety and bravery, he believed that we could all achieve wisdom. He stated that virtue was the most valuable thing anyone could have and it is still something that many believe in today.

Socrates Cautioned Us of the Foolishness of Materialism

Socrates was not a big fan of splashing out money for extravagant things. He was described as wearing only one tattered cloak throughout the year and didn't wear sandals. As a result, his peers would often laugh at him for this but Socrates refused to listen. For him, his modest appearance was a reflection of his notion that excessive materialism would not bring happiness, just ignorance. Socrates stated that the Athenians would enrich themselves by seeking true happiness instead of material wealth – something that continues to be applicable in today's commercial culture.

We Learned the Value of Civil Disobedience

Socrates was often referred to as the gadfly of Athens in that it was his job to sting the government into improving the parts of how it ran the state. Socrates had no issue in standing up and speaking his mind when it came to a poorly run government, even if it came to a heavy price. Socrates was mentioned by Martin Luther King, a man famous across the world for civil disobedience, in his letter from prison back in the early 1960s. 2,500 years may have separated Socrates and King, and five decades between King and today, but still just as relevant.

We Learned that it Is Important to Stand Up for What We Believe In

Socrates live his life according to his beliefs and philosophy, even when they were derided, laughed at, mocked and were frightened of, and eventually died defending them. The government of his day brought charges against him, claiming that he was trying to introduce new gods and corrupt the youth. In 309 BCE, he was found guilty and ordered to commit suicide by drinking hemlock. The accusations brought against him may have been a cover to disguise the political motivations of those bringing the charges, since the amnesty of 403 BCE forbade prosecution for political transgressions committed before that date.

Socrates had every opportunity at his trial to renounce his beliefs, to swear that he would not corrupt the youth, to submit towards the state or even to go into exile with his family (Socrates was married to Xanthippe and had two sons). Yet he did not do this. Instead, he argued against the charges and even went so far to judge those who had found him guilty of impiety. Socrates continues to stand up for what he believed in, even when it cost him his life. While many scholars have suggested that Socrates has a touch of the martyr when it came to his death, it is still inspirational to see someone who believes in their cause so much that they were willing to die for it. We have seen this throughout history and in today's society, when it is so simple to take the easy way out of a hard situation, it shows us that we too can stand up for something we believe in passionately.

Chapter 12: Timeless Sayings of Socrates

Socrates, the classical Greek philosopher, has been credited with the foundation of Western philosophy. The renowned figure's work has been predominantly revealed through the writings of his students, Xenophon and Plato, and the plays of Aristophanes. Born circa 470 BC in Athens, Greece, little is known of Socrates's life outside of his philosophy. However, it is known that Socrates had a wife and fathered three sons. He inherited the profession of his father, as most men did in those times, but he gave it up to be a philosopher. Socrates believed that the ultimate goal of philosophy was to establish a greater well-being of society as a whole. He taught his work to the young men who managed to carry on the legacy he created. With the "Socratic Method", Socrates developed the foundation for Western systems of logic, ethics, and philosophy.

Though he existed over 2000 years ago, many of Socrates famous quotes remain wildly relevant to this day, and can be effortlessly implemented into modern, everyday life. Society has changed significantly since those times, but the basic principles remain. His quotes may also have multiple meanings, still relevant in today's society. For example, Socrates once said, "True knowledge exists in knowing that you know nothing". This profound quote could mean that to have an understanding that you essentially know nothing leaves you the room to gather genuine intelligence. The same quote can also mean that knowing that you know nothing makes you intelligent because discoveries are made on a daily basis. These discoveries often disprove previous truths. Similarly, Socrates stated, "I know that I am intelligent, because I know that I know nothing." As we have seen throughout this book, Socrates believed a state of initial admitted ignorance to be essential to the development of true knowledge. Before embarking upon the accumulation of wisdom in any subject, it was (according to Socrates) essential to admit that you were in fact ignorant of that subject. By starting with a blank slate, it's possible to enter into the process of learning with no predilections or presumptions. This allows for the acquisition of real, lasting knowledge, and keeps us from reacting defensively whenever we're presented with a piece of information that contradict our preconceived notions.

Another enlightening Socrates saying is, "If a man would move the world, he must first move himself." This quote refers to the fact that if a person wants to make a change in the world, they must first embody the change they want to make. "False words are not only evil in themselves, but they infect the soul with evil," is another fundamental Socrates quote, stating that telling lies is not only harmful in general, but also negatively affects the person telling them. Socrates strongly stood behind his saying, "To find yourself, think for yourself." This is a testament to the notion that self-discovery comes from forming your own thoughts and ideas, rather than being influenced by outside sources or groups. So many of these quotes should be applied to modern times. Socrates's teachings could make great improvements in our society if they were adopted into our daily lives.

"True Knowledge Exists In Knowing That You Know Nothing."

This timeless saying can be applied to life today, and for eternity. Though the words seem to contradict themselves, the meaning behind them is harmonious. In a world where so much knowledge is available to us through education, books, television, and even our peers, it seems nonsensical to say that true knowledge is equal to having no knowledge at all. This quote, however, refers to a much deeper sense of knowledge. In our immense universe, it is impossible to know absolutely everything. There is always room for learning, growth, and understanding. Socrates was immensely humble in his quest for knowledge, always listening to others, seeking new sources of information, and keeping an open mind. To succumb to the idea that you know virtually nothing of the world will open your eyes to its depth and vastness, bestowing you with true knowledge. When one admits to not knowing, or having little knowledge of a subject, it motivates him to listen to others, discover other sources of information, and remain open to outside facts and opinions. When Socrates referred to "knowing nothing", it seems he meant that true knowledge comes from being intellectually humble.

Socrates made the similar statement, "I know that I am intelligent, because I know that I know nothing," which is another testament to being intellectually humble. Though the concept of being humble seems especially simple, it typically takes a conscious effort to apply this idea in day-to-day life. Many of the world's most horrific tragedies have been the product of people who were too stubborn or set in their own ways to bend in their thinking or see their own wrongdoings. Numerous evil dictators believed, without a doubt, that certain groups or people were the cause of their country's hardship. This certainty often led to mass genocide, war, and other horrific incidents. It is likely that many of these events could have been avoided if these single-minded leaders had a sense of intellectual humility.

In the Socrates's famous quote, to "know nothing" does not mean to be dimwitted or naïve. True knowledge derives from the willingness to learn. Applying this saying in our real lives may take a conscious effort, but it is applicable in countless situations that most of us face every day. The work place is a great example of where this thoughtful saying can be applied. While you may initially disagree with a colleague's techniques and procedures, adopting a sense of intellectual humility and trying to understand your colleague's way will ultimately leave you with newfound knowledge. You may discover you prefer your colleague's methods of executing work. You may find your own method is more efficient, or you might find that fusing the techniques produce the best results. In a disagreement with a friend or loved one, listening carefully and gathering more information through a question and answer process is another instance where you may implement this saying into daily life. When arguing, it is natural to get defensive and combative, but accepting that you "know nothing" of where the other person is coming from emotionally, is likely to ease tension and produce a positive resolution more quickly. Listening to the other person and developing an understanding of where the thoughts, feelings and opinions expressed stem from, can help you find the sense of forgiveness or empathy necessary to settle the argument.

In a school setting, Socrates's thoughtful saying is incredibly applicable. Much of Socrates own education was developed through discussion, Q&A, critical thinking, and spending time with his contemporaries. Socrates stood by his statement by remaining wholly open to the ideas of others, and to the notion that knowledge can be uncovered everywhere and at any time. It is exceptionally helpful to allow the idea that you know very little to motivate you to learn more, especially when immersing yourself in an educational setting. In a college setting, there are many more sources for learning than the course material alone. Professors, other students, books, and plays are endless sources of knowledge, even when their teachings do not seem obvious. Most students follow exactly what they are taught in school, only learning from that single source. By participating in other educational activities, students can learn beyond what they are taught in school, and knowledge is one of the most powerful tools available to us.

"I Know That I Am Intelligent, Because I Know That I Know Nothing."

This statement is not a confession of stupidity, but a confirmation of intelligence. Maintaining the awareness and wisdom that you know essentially nothing will eternally encourage you to go out and discover more. Those who have come to a mental place where they believe they know it all often miss out on the wondrous, mind-altering experiences life has to offer. The ability to change your perspective, or understand things from a different perspective while maintaining your own ideas is a valuable quality to have. This trait can often be attributed to personal success and happiness. Facts change everyday due to scientific discoveries. For example, it was once believed that the world was flat. Those who challenged this idea were persecuted by society. Explorers eventually discovered that those who were being persecuted were actually correct. When it was discovered that the world was in fact round, many found that those who challenged the common beliefs were actually the most intelligent people because they considered other options.

Closed-mindedness frequently results in the loss of relationships, failure and bitterness. By remaining open-minded and humble, Socrates became one of the most inspiring and influential philosophers of all time. Consciously developing a mindset of intellectual humility and open-mindedness can very likely improve your quality of life, your work, and your relationships. Again, accepting that you know very little is not a shameful admission, but a humble approach to a remarkable journey of never-ending intellectual growth. Being a person who is teachable results in many opportunities that may not be available to the close-minded or arrogant. The open-minded are able to truly immerse themselves in education with no preconceived notions that hinder them from gathering new and exciting information every day.

Exploring just about anything outside of the self can be much more accessible when coming from a standpoint of knowing nothing. Those who explore other cultures can better understand the inner workings of the people, traditions and lifestyles involved when they do not harbor the idea that their own culture has taught them everything there is to know about how to live. Those who delve into the medicinal field can more easily develop new and alternative options when approaching their studies with a mind that is not anchored to outdated rules or traditions. Those who make art or music can greatly benefit from creating with no tainted perceptions of what art is supposed to be, or what music should sound like. Those who choose to approach science from a standpoint of knowing nothing can more readily spot new methods and systems that may have gone unnoticed by predecessors that were stuck on a certain set of rules or ideas. Socrates approached the study of philosophy from a place of knowing nothing and thus developed practical ideas, methods and foundations that continued to be used in the study of the subject to this day. Had Socrates not adopted a sense of intellectual humility, Western philosophy would be much different today.

This is something that applies a lot in society today. After proving and disproving so many common theories, people have become more open to new knowledge. Thanks to this, helpful new discoveries are made everyday. The open-mindedness of people today have allowed us to make countless medical and scientific discoveries that have saved and improved the lives of just about everyone in the world. If people were still as closed-minded as they once were, then we would not have half of the life-saving medical technologies that we have today. Knowing that you do not know everything allows room for new ideas and theories to take root in your mind. Not everyone in the world is open-minded, but the irony is that those who think they know everything are the ones who are constantly proven to be wrong.

"To Find Yourself, Think For Yourself."

This Socrates quote is basically saying that in order to know who you are, you have to be free from the influence of others. When you follow the choices of others without considering how you feel about the choices you are making, and let them influence your decisions, you are not being yourself. In fact, you are allowing the personalities of others to overshadow your own. Over time, doing this may cause you to not even know who you are as a person. In order to find out who you are, you have to think and act by your own will, and not let the pressure of others push you into doing things you may not have done without the pressure of your peers, elders or anyone else who may influence your decisions. This is important because thinking for yourself and acting on what you believe is right is what makes you an individual.

The main trait that this quote is getting across is "individuality". Society often urges people to conform. Whatever personality traits were popular at the time are the ones that everyone tends to try and imitate. By conforming to what is considered popular, you are losing your identity. While attempting to blend in, many people make poor decisions that are influenced by peers. These decisions often lead to negative consequences that can have long-term effects on your life. For example, if the "cool" thing at the time is to do drugs, and you do them even though you know it is wrong, so many bad things can happen. You can overdose, end up in legal trouble, or even get addicted. Things like this can change who you are into someone you don't even recognize. This sort of scenario happens all the time with actors. They get so immersed into their roles that they take on characteristics of the characters they play and as a result they begin to lose parts of themselves. Keeping your individuality sometimes means standing up to others by saying "no" when they are pressuring you to do something that you know is wrong. Unfortunately, sometimes this may cause people to turn their backs on you, but those who truly are your friends will respect you for embracing your individuality and making your own choices. Individuality is the most important part of a person because it is what makes everyone different and it is what makes you the person you are.

Applying this to your everyday life can be difficult, especially for a teenager or young adult when friendship and popularity are such important parts of life. People who are actually friends will respect you for making your own choices and some may even follow you in doing the same thing. To maintain your individuality it is important to accept yourself for who you are, flaws and all. You must also expect others to accept you and respect that you make your own decisions. Avoid trying to impress people because this is when you are more likely to do things that you wouldn't normally do. You know what is right and wrong, everyone has a moral compass. The reason it is there is to help you make the right decisions. Embrace it, if you feel something is wrong then don't do it. Respect the choices of others to do what they feel is right, but do not compromise your own values in order to satisfy someone else. Here is a scenario that perfectly embodies the concept of individuality. You and a friend stay up all night having fun. An assignment is due the next day, so your friend plagiarizes the assignment. She tries to get you to do the same and you choose not to. Instead, you decide to be honest with the teacher. Not only are you staying true to your morals, but you are setting a good example for your friend to follow. Staying true to yourself means doing what you feel is right, and that is the only way you will discover who you are.

An obstacle that may come with applying this principle is self-confidence. Without confidence it can be hard to make your own decisions because people without confidence usually strive to become someone else. As a result, they make decisions that they think the person they want to become would make, even when they know it is wrong. Insecurity will push you to allow others to control your decisions. You can beat this by accepting your flaws, and even embracing them. Confidence breeds the courage it takes to stand up for what you believe. If you know that your opinion of yourself matters much more than the opinion of others, then you are less likely to conform to others due to your insecurities. Standing up for yourself, and watching the respect you will gain, will help to boost your confidence so that you don't have to feel insecure about being who you are.

This concept is necessary to a functional and progressive society. People conform easily to others, which causes everyone to adopt the same opinions, even if those opinions are wrong. If no one is different then no one questions those opinions and they become considered fact. The point of having a diverse society is that everyone is different. We all have our own opinions and we can all learn from the opinions of others. If everyone conformed, then nothing would ever be challenged. As a result, no new knowledge would ever be discovered. In order to make advances, we need people who think differently. People who will question what is considered to be true. It is these people that make us change our ways of thinking over time, which helps us advance and discover more knowledge. A world where everyone is the same would be a very dull world.

"False Words Are Not Only Evil In Themselves, But They Infect The Soul With Evil."

This Socrates quote is making the point that lies can be very hurtful to all parties involved. This is what makes them evil. Lies are not only evil in themselves, but they create a larger evil over time. Lies are hurtful and destructive to relationships on their own. Not only do they hurt others, but they also harm the one telling the lie. The damage caused by one lie can continue forever until the truth finally comes out. Telling one lie can cause you to tell many more to cover up the first lie. Even if you have good intentions behind the lie, the lies can continue on until your good intentions become lost in all of the lies that are told in order to keep the first lie from coming out into the open. Once you begin telling the lies, it becomes easier to continue lying over time. This can have negative effects on your moral compass as the lies come more easily. One lie can start a snowball effect to the point where there are lies coming in almost every conversation you have.

The big lesson that this quote revolves around is the importance of honesty. After telling so many lies, lying can become a habit. This can lead a person to the point where they have become what we call a compulsive liar. This is when people begin telling lies without even realizing or caring about the truth. Like the quote says, lying can infect your soul. The truth is the only way to cure the infection. If the lies have gotten out of hand, telling the truth can break the habit of lying. Many of us tell ourselves elaborate excuses so that lying seems like the right thing to do. It may be to avoid hurting someone or to avoid getting hurt ourselves, but either way, lying is wrong. Being honest will result in a much better overall outcome. At times it does seem like honesty will destroy our relationships, but most people are more capable of forgiving if the truth is told, than if a lie is told and the truth comes out involuntarily. For example, if you have committed a crime and you go before the judge and tell the truth, then the court system is more likely to take mercy on you and you may get a lighter punishment. However, if you lie, try to cover it up and the truth comes out anyway, then the judge will be more likely to give you the maximum punishment allowable under the law. Lies normally do come out in the end, so it is best to just get it over with and be truthful from the beginning. Telling the truth establishes trust.

Applying this to your life is easy, if you haven't already gotten into the habit of lying. If you have, then it may be a bit more difficult. If you haven't gotten into the habit of lies, then just keep being truthful, and fighting urges to cover up the truth when you've made a mistake. On the other hand, those who have gotten into a lying habit must rectify their lies. They must initiate a conversation with the loved one or loved ones with whom they've been dishonest, and explain the situation. Explain how the lies started and why, and remember to be one hundred percent truthful. As you begin letting the truth come out, it is likely that it will get easier to tell the truth. Being truthful will come more naturally, and most of the people you have lied to will likely forgive you over time. Regaining the trust of others can be the biggest obstacle you face when breaking your lying habit. Loved ones may not have the faith in you that they once did. You have to earn this back over time by continuing to be honest, even when you know the truth may be painful to hear. Being honest may cause a bit of pain at first, but consider the alternative before telling a lie. That one lie will turn into many, and all of the lies will likely come out eventually. At that point you have hurt the person ten times more because not only did you make a mistake, but you then told hundreds of lies to cover it up.

Being a compulsive liar has many consequences that could make you think twice the next time you have the urge to tell a lie. Once you are caught in so many lies, people stop trusting you, and they no longer believe anything you say. Have you ever heard the story of the boy who cried wolf? This cautionary children's tale can easily turn into a real life scenario. If you are caught in hundreds of lies by your friends and family, it becomes impossible for them to believe you. Then when you are telling the truth, no one believes it because of your constant lies. For example, if you lie about the reason you need money when you borrow money from friends, then they are likely to stop lending money to you. Then, when you really need the money, they don't believe you because of all your previous lies, and you suffer as a result. In situations like this it takes time and effort to regain the trust you lost. You have to redeem yourself to everyone you have lied to.

Lying has become like second nature to many people in society today. There are even careers that pretty much revolve around lies and half-truths. Most people are skeptical and distrustful of everyone because of how natural lying has become. It has gotten to the point where it has become difficult to give money to the man on the side of the road begging, because in many cases that man has more money to his name than you do. Many charities have the same bad reputation because only pennies on the dollar actually go to the cause you are donating to. This is not the case with all charities, but the ones that are being dishonest tend to give a bad name to all charities due to the constant lies told by people and organizations. This has led us to become a very distrustful society. We need to embrace honesty so that the constant distrust can stop. Even those few who are honest people suffer because of the general dishonesty in our society today.

"If A Man Would Move The World, He Must First Move Himself."

This reflective quote refers to humankind and their desire to make a change in the world. This saying remains incredibly applicable to present day life, and the matters of making change. Like many of his other sayings, the meaning behind this quote is simplistic, yet wildly profound. When a person decides to make a change, he must first implement a change in himself. This testament is true in situations both big and small. If someone wants more kindness in the workplace, first he must be kind in the workplace himself. If a mean and bitter person wanted to see more kindness in the workplace, yet continued to be mean and bitter to his colleagues, it is highly unlikely that a change would ever take place. Change starts within the self, and only then can it spread to the others around you.

The world's most influential leaders embodied the change they sought to make before prompting a shift in others. Martin Luther King changed the course of history by leaps and bounds with the efforts he made for the Civil Rights movement. Before presenting his ideas for change to others, Martin Luther King practiced the changes he wished to see in society. His simple act of embodying the difference, he wanted to make deeply affected the nation's people and history. This testament also rings true for other Human Rights Activists such as Mahatma Gandhi, Mother Teresa, Eleanor Roosevelt, and Nelson Mandela.

Of course, this statement does not only apply to matters of activism and civil rights. This saying has remained pertinent over hundreds of years because of its flexibility. This quote can be applied to making change in any context. "Moving the world" can be as simple as making a difference in your family's everyday lifestyle. If you would like to see the members of your household help each other with daily tasks more often, start by helping the members of your household yourself. If you would like to see your community reduce its waste, start by recycling at home or joining a community compost pile. Small changes can eventually lead to bigger changes, but change can never take place on a larger scale if it does not take place within you first. This saying is also conducive to anyone looking to make an advancement in their personal life. Whether you are looking for a career path, a promotion, a relationship, or a spiritual awakening, it is useless to think these developments will take place without first taking action yourself. Many people who seek a career path start by seeking a higher education. Those who want to be promoted in their field start by working harder and smarter in the positions they currently hold. People who seek relationships often start by branching outside of their social circle and meeting new people in situations outside of their comfort zone. Those who seek a spiritual awakening or enlightenment will plan trips, attend church, or explore meditation.

The idea of "moving the world" is defined by the person who looks to take action. Each person's world, and their perception of what needs to be changed to make their world a better place, is different. When Socrates said, "If a man would move the world, he must first move himself," he was not necessarily referring to the entire globe, but someone who desires to change the world can certainly take the quote for face value. However, someone looking to change the world must implement the same basic steps as someone who is simply looking to change his daily lifestyle. In both situations, the change begins within. Changing the world is a feasible achievement when you demonstrate the change you want to make in every aspect of your life. There are many ways to "move the world", and countless people have done so, and continue to do so using this same principle that Socrates both practiced and stood by. Someone who wants to better the environment can start by building an environmentally friendly lifestyle for himself. A musician who wants to make a change in the industry can start by writing the songs he wants to hear on the radio. A politician who wants to help the people of a nation achieve a better quality of life can start by helping those in his or her own community. The possibilities to invoke change in your personal life, your work life, and even the entire world are endless, so long as the change begins with you. It is easy to point out what changes might improve your world without making an effort to make a difference. Many people spend hours speculating adjustments the government should or should not make to improve the lives of a nation's citizens, but most of them fail to assimilate the differences they'd like to see in their own lives. People will often expect kindness, respect and love from their significant others while treating the person with disrespect and rudeness. This type of hypocrisy will oftentimes root itself as an unconscious habit in the human mind, preventing positive change and resulting in bitterness and animosity. Making a conscious effort to break away from this hypocrisy takes dedication, but your effort is bound to move your world in the direction you want it to go.

Getting involved in the causes you stand by, treating others how you want to be treated, and taking action towards a better quality of life are all infallible examples of "moving yourself" in order to "move the world". Embracing your values and putting them into action will inspire others to join the cause, which can create a larger movement and in turn, move the world. Changing the world can start with an action as basic as recycling a newspaper, being more kind to your co-workers, planting a tree, attending a political rally, or lending a helping hand to a family member. Making an effort where you may not have made an effort in the past is the first step to making a difference. Socrates ultimate goal was to better the well-being of society, and by first bettering himself, he went on to better society with his crucial contributions to Western philosophy.

"Beauty Is A Short-Lived Tyranny."

How does this apply to modern man today? Universally, humanity pursues outward beauty beyond its reasonable limits. Our social status greatly depends on outward beauty. This makes beauty a sort of tyranny. To avoid losing the social status that beauty provides, we go to extreme lengths. We try to preserve our beauty well into our later years. Plastic surgery is a perfect example of how we sculpt our faces and smooth out the wrinkles that have developed because of natural aging. New products are available that claim to preserve beauty. No amount of surgeries or products will preserve that beauty forever. Socrates is right in that beauty is a short-lived tyranny because we cannot preserve it forever. Sooner or later everyone on this planet is going to grow old and lose their outward beauty. When that beauty is lost, so are the benefits that come with it.

Does a person's real value lie in the depth of the outer beauty they possess? I recall seeing a Betty Davis movie where she was the finest looking women of her time. All the men wanted to be around her and with her. Men would fall over themselves just to get a piece of attention from her. She would get anyone and anything she wanted. Whenever she walked into a room, all the male eyes would gravitate and hang on her every move, word, and action. All of her relationships were shallow with no real substance to them. Why? Because it was based on a superficial premise - her elegant looks. Did these men care about the real person who lived within? Probably not! Her outer beauty bought her all the things she wanted. Though eventually the beauty went away with age, but what was on the inside did not.

Of course, all the women disliked her because she was so outwardly beautiful and desired by all men. Women were jealous of her beauty. Then low and behold, she was tragically struck by a facial disease that aged her and carved up her beautiful face. This left her with unsightly visible scars. No plastic surgery could restore her beauty or even come close to erasing the effects of the disease. Unfortunately, she didn't realize that "Beauty is short-lived tyranny." She went everywhere still expecting to be treated as the glowing, privileged beauty she once was. People no longer gazed lovingly at her when she walked into the room, and women no longer envied her great looks. Men were no longer hung in droves by her side. Men and women still stared at her, but for a different reason. She had lost her beauty, and she was now outwardly homely. Men would talk about her, but not like they used to. They would talk about how they couldn't believe how unsightly she had become. Women still didn't like her, but now they were gloating over her lost beauty.

As her beauty disintegrated, men stopped asking her out and paying attention to her. She was once the talk of the town, now she had become a fallen angel. She had no more friends and lost her magnetism over the male species. It took her awhile, but she realized that outward beauty is fleeting and temporal. Outward beauty comes and goes, the beauty that you have inside remains. It just goes to show that you can lose your physical beauty at any time. It is important not to put too much value on your outward beauty, because doing so can have an adverse effect on your inner beauty. It is very easy to become conceited and shallow. If that outward beauty is what makes a person who they are, and it is lost in a tragic accident, then what do you have left? Beauty doesn't last, so make sure you have other redeeming qualities. Today, people still try to pursue that ever-elusive fountain of youth. Yes, society reacts differently to good-looking people, but is this valuing a human being for who they are? Men and women try all sorts of modern techniques (plastic surgery, liposuction, organic anti-aging creams and many other sources) to maintain that outward youthful, beautiful luster. But is this really who they are? Sooner or later, old age will catch up with them and they won't be able to stay ahead of its effects. In time, aging does catch up with these people, they are only known for their outward beauty and any influence they have in society is lost. Those who retain their influence are those who are known for their intelligence or kindness. People that have inner beauty retain their influence, even after the outer beauty has been snuffed out by old age or tragedy.

Another tyranny of beauty is power. It's true, "beautiful people" have power over other people. The more beautiful you are, the greater the hold you have on people. But even this influence will pass away as you begin to age and lose your natural, outward beauty. When you're beautiful, you always have to wonder if your relationship is real and based on love or if the love will fade when your looks do. In many cases, when the beauty is gone, so is the friendship. Worse yet, what happens when a couple is attracted to one another because of outward beauty? They get married and think they are in love with the "whole" person - body, soul and spirit. But are they? Or are they just in love with each other's physical beauty? So, what happens when the outward beauty of either spouse disintegrates? Over time, when the effects of aging kick in and our physical beauty fades. The logical conclusion will be the marriage will fall apart and unravel because the shallow foundation it was built on has crumbled.

Could another tyranny of beauty be that people who are considered to have outstanding looks be favored unfairly over individuals who aren't as good-looking? Even to the point that these people are discriminated against? It is a sad truth, but yes, there is discrimination in every culture of every nation on this planet. Good-looking people are hired for jobs they aren't technically qualified for because they are more beautiful than other applicants. Needless to say, the qualified candidates are passed over because they are plainer looking. It is part of human nature to be more drawn to physical beauty. In fact, a study was conducted that showed even infants and young children are drawn more to physically attractive people than they are to those who lack what is considered physical beauty.

I heard of a case several years ago, where a young woman was pursuing a lifelong dream of becoming a flight attendant. She went and applied for the job, and she was turned down. She was young, vibrant and qualified for the position. Why was she turned down? The particular airline said she was too ugly to be a flight attendant and passed her over. How did she feel about not being beautiful enough for the job? In many cases (not always), people with extraordinary outward beauty may be very self-absorbed and shallow. It could come to the point where they choose their friends and spouses based on how they rate on the looks scale from 1-10! The good-looking standard leaves the beautiful people in a one-dimensional place. All of their relationships are based on the fleeting level of outward beauty. I guarantee they will forge no lifelong lasting relationships based on this criterion.

They are robbing themselves of fruitful and profound friendships they could have had with people who are plainer looking in their perspective. We must look beyond just surface beauty to find the real worth of a person. Don't think that a good-looking person is necessarily shallow. You know, some of the finest looking people in the world today are the ones that outwardly radiate an unmistakable inward beauty! Socrates saw the actual nature of humanity when he made this famous quote: "Beauty is a short-lived tyranny." The truth of this quote is imminent. Outer beauty will not last like inner beauty will. Applying this quote to your life means focusing on your inner beauty rather than your outer beauty. It is not wrong to feel confident in your outer beauty, but do not let it outshine the qualities that make you beautiful within.

"By All Means Marry; If You Get A Good Wife, You'll Be Happy. If You Get A Bad One, You'll Become A Philosopher. "

Did Socrates make this controversial quote? Some philosophy experts say they couldn't find any sources to verify he originated this saying. So let's assume Socrates did make the quote. What did he mean by "By all means marry; if you get a good wife, you'll be happy. If you get a bad one, you'll become a philosopher. Did Socrates become a philosopher because he married a bad wife? Or was he happy because he married a good wife and became a philosopher anyway? How does this quote apply to us today where divorce seems to be as common as going to the supermarket? If this quote does belong to Socrates, it certainly seems as if he is saying that he got a bad wife. Not to mention, there are many claims that Socrates and his wife did not have a healthy marriage, but in those times divorce was unheard of, so they may have been stuck with one another whether they liked it or not.

Socrates could have been talking about reflecting on how your wife became bad, or that she was bad from day one. He could have had divorce in mind when he made this statement. How many men, after how many divorces may have sat around wondering what went wrong in his marriage? He marries the perfect woman and then six months, maybe a year later, they get divorced because of incompatibility. He wonders what went so wrong that he would end up in a divorce. They had so much in common in the early years of their relationship, he thought they would be so happy for the rest of their lives. Upon deeper reflection, he begins to analyze the deeper root causes of why they ended up splitting forever. It often happens that people do not really know each other until they are married and living under one roof. For so many couples, that is when it seems to begin to go wrong.

A failed marriage often leaves people wondering where the seemingly perfect marriage went wrong. Did his drug and alcohol addiction have anything to do with the marriage going south? He thinks about how he spent thousands of dollars to maintain his addictions. His wife pleaded and begged him to stop spending all their money on his unhealthy habits. He remembers how he overdosed on cocaine that one fateful November day. His wife rushed him to the hospital, and he almost died. Then the next month he drank so much he began hitting her and physically abusing her to the point she had to leave and go to a homeless shelter for battered women. Scenarios like this are not at all uncommon in today's society. Fortunately, all of the men that this happens to do not become philosophers, because in that case, we would have a lot of modern day philosophers.

Once the marriage is over, the reflection sets in and both parties wonder where it went wrong and what they both could, or should have done differently. He thinks about how they had to file for bankruptcy because of his chronic drug habit. He spent all of their savings, then he went through their retirement funds. The saddest part was when he started to use his paychecks to buy the drugs instead of buying food and paying the mortgage. Could these reasons be why his wife became a "bad" wife, and he became a philosopher? Both people in a marriage can influence the personalities of the other. Bad behavior from one party can fuel similar behavior from the other. Relationships are build on mutual respect and trust, and without this, they feed off each other's shortcomings.

What about a middle of the road scenario? In this case, the husband marries a good wife and then things change between them in their relationship due to the shortcomings of one party or both. She becomes a bad wife to him, and he is now a philosopher. Both of them do things that are destructive to the relationship and then they eventually hit a realization that they need to fix their strained relationship. Down the road, she once again becomes a good wife due to the realizations of their mistakes and the efforts that follow to repair the broken relationship. We can catch this man reflecting on how his marriage went from good to bad, then back to good again. Let's listen in on his thoughts. He begins at the point where the marriage went bad: He begins some dark (I mean deep soul searching.)

Could the cause of the change in her behavior be due to the two illicit affairs he had during the first five years of their marriage? They were so happy together in those early years. His thinking changed about his relationship with his wife. Maybe the young female co-worker would be more exciting than his annoying wife. He couldn't stop thinking about that tantalizing, young, sexy co-worker who always seemed to be hanging out at his desk all day long. She wore clothes that took his mind into realms he shouldn't have entered. She just wore him down with provocative invites day after day. "Why don't you come over to my place after work for a drink? You know I am a great cook so let me cook you a cozy dinner after work tonight. Give your wife the standard excuse that you have to work late this evening. You are just thinking of her and the kids. You know you want to get ahead and provide a better life for your children." He remembers how her many persuasions finally wore him down. Those occasional late nights at the office turned into a nightly affair, then transformed into a regular Saturday afternoon thing, as well. He even started working to get ahead on Sundays to get that big promotion that would set his family up for life. He thinks about how his wife was comfortable with his "overtime" at first. But months went by and the paychecks never changed and the promotion never materialized. He started to become distant from her. He couldn't stand being around her after a while. Eventually, she caught on that he was having an affair, but she couldn't divorce him because it went against her deepest moral convictions. She became unbearable, always asking him where he was going and who he was with.

The first breaking point came when he began talking about divorce and how he was not in love with her anymore. She finally confronted him about the affair. Of course, he adamantly denied it at first. Finally, he broke down and admitted to the affair. Naturally, she was crushed, but she was still willing to try again and make it work. So they went through some counseling and seemingly restored the relationship. But his affair patterns began again. By the second time she had enough. She left him and began divorce proceedings. She had made up her mind and refused to put up with him any longer. The split wasn't easy. She was lonely and depressed, the pain and rejection was just too much to bear. She attempted to commit suicide.

Then he thought about how thankful he was that he found her on the living room floor, still breathing, and rushed her to the hospital. They were able to pump her stomach and get all the poison out before it became fatal! The lights finally came on, and he realized why she had become a bad wife, and how hurt she was by his actions. He had put her through the pain and rejection of two extramarital affairs. He realized that in her mind, the affairs were worse than divorce. He had rejected her in the most intimate and deepest way possible.

He remembers the emotional and fragile reunion they had in the hospital room. He wondered if she could find the strength to give him another chance. Graciously, she agreed to take him back a third time YES A THIRD TIME! He turned his behavior around and never looked at another woman again. He realized her love for him was for better or for worse (In this case, it was terrible!) She came as close to showing him unconditional love as a human could. He would never forget what he put her through and in the end, she still stood by his side. Don't be fooled, their relationship had to be rebuilt and the trust that was buried deep between them had to be developed again. He is now secure in his marriage, knowing she will never leave or cheat on him. Against all human odds, she fully trusts him again. So in this marriage, he did have a good wife, and he is happy. He is also a philosopher.

I know of a case where a husband wasn't so fortunate with his marriage. She bore him three children and was genuinely in love with this man. They moved to another state, and he began to become distant from her, and he showed signs of being unfaithful to her. Her suspicions were right, and she found out he was having an extramarital affair. She forgave him for his transgression and took him back in as her soulmate and the father her children. The marriage seemed to be on healthy and stable ground again. They even had another child together. They moved back to the state I currently live in and appeared to flourish. Lo and behold, he cheated on her again. You would think the marriage wouldn't survive this second breach, but it did. She took him back a second time. I lost contact with this couple, but I ran into her a few years later. Unbelievably, he had a third affair! This time, it was too much strain on their relationship, and she booted him out of the house and divorced him. Was she a "bad wife" for divorcing him after a third extramarital affair? He may be thinking she was because she didn't take him back a third time. He also may be thinking she was a "bad" wife in the first place that drove him to have the first affair, then the second and finally the third. She put up with more than any wife should. She could have divorced him after the first affair. She didn't and stuck with him through two affairs. The third one was too much for her to forgive. She was a good wife that put up with more than her share of grief. What would Socrates say in this situation?

"Children Today Are Tyrants. They Contradict Their Parents, Gobble Their Food, And Tyrannize Their Teachers."

The quote describes children born and raised in every generation since the beginning of time. What Socrates says describes children raised in our day and age. Children are naturally selfish. In the beginning stages of life they only think about their own wants and needs. Empathy for others is something that is developed over time, as parents and role models teach these concepts to children. In a case where the children are not taught correctly, you see children blamed 100% for this universal type of behavior. Parents are supposed to set the rules and be the primary role models for their children from the time of their birth. They set down the control from day one. The parents must instill self-discipline and self-control in their children and teach them proper moral principles at the appropriate stages in life.

The children of every generation will be the products of their parent's upbringing. Parents must teach their children to respect their parents, then it will naturally follow that they learn to respect other authority figures. Like their grandparent's, school teachers, church leaders such as youth pastors or Sunday school teachers. They learn to respect other human beings and to treat them like they want to be treated. They learn to respect the property and opinions of others. They will appreciate other cultural differences in appearance, and learn to accept everyone as a human being, no matter what race or nationality they are. In order for children to understand all of these concepts, parents must instill values in their children. Without the proper teachings and discipline, children will always be tyrants.

If the children are tyrants in public settings such as school, the boy scouts or at birthday parties, etc., it's because the parents lost control over their children years ago. It starts with a little temper tantrum in the store over a pack of gum. The child asks for a pack of gum and the parent says "no." The child starts to whine, but the mother stands firm and says "no" again. The child starts yelling, yet the parent still says no. Then the kid blows over into a full fledged tantrum, screaming and yelling. He starts rolling on the ground! Now the kid holds his breath, and he is turning purple from lack of air. The parent finally breaks down and buys the child the controversial pack of gum. The battle and the war has been lost. The next time the child and the parent are in the store, the power play happens again. This time, the stakes are a little higher - the kid wants an ice cream cone. Here comes the predictable behavior again. The child asks for the ice cream cone, and the parent says no. The kid raises his voice a little, so the parent gives in (fearing an embarrassing public display and being accused of being a bad mother.) So starts the tyranny of the child at a very young age. He learns that if he engages in inappropriate behavior, he can take control of the situation and the person(s) involved. He has no sense of when he is disrespecting his parents or anyone else around.

The child then moves on to the next stage of Socrates's saying "They contradict their parents." At this point, the child has lost all respect for his parents and adult authority figures in general. The child now has blurred the lines in the household as to who is in charge. The parents have lost control of the child to the point that now the child calls the shots. The child has plainly become self-governing because he can now do whatever he wants. He will now contradict everything the parents say, think and do. He will talk in abusive tones and verbally abuse his parents in everyday conversations. Naturally, this behavior will carry over into all of the child's relationships, primarily adult connections. He has learned all he has to do is throw a tantrum, and he will get what he wants. He has become a master manipulator over other people.

The part about the children gobbling their food is a result of children not being taught proper eating habits and manners early in life. They start out young, developing poor eating habits because parents let them eat whatever they want, whenever they want, and however they want. They never set down guidelines or taught the children proper eating mannerisms. Or, maybe they tried to teach the children healthy eating habits, but the child resisted the attempts by the parents, and the fight was on. The parents try to keep order at the table, but kids rebel against the rules. You see, the child has already learned that if he throws a fit when his parents won't buy him what he wants, that they will give in to him. So, when they try to instruct him on proper table manners, the same thing happens. If they try to teach him how to hold a fork correctly, take small bites and not talk with his mouth full of food, the kid again uses the tantrum technique, and his parents cave again.

Today, teachers have to be so careful how they discipline and interact with their students. If they grab a kid's arm or put their hand on his shoulder, they can be slapped with an abuse charge, taken to court and sued for all kinds of money. The school could get sued and lose its good standing in the community. Ultimately, the teacher could lose his or her job. This being said, a child who has learned to control his parents will have no problem controlling and tyrannizing his teachers. The kid acts disrespectfully in class, and if the teacher makes any move to discipline or control the disruptive student, the student cries "abuse" or accuses the teacher of unfair treatment. The student has learned how to manipulate the teacher and he has control over the coach. The tyranny has begun, and the student can do whatever he wants.

So, what we can learn from this Socrates quote is that the parent has to maintain control and not give in to the child in the early stages of parenting. If a parent steadily gives into the child, then over time the child will expect to get everything he or she wants by being rude and rebellious. It is important that parents guide their children by encouraging them to do good, praising them when they do, and disciplining them when they misbehave. Then the child learns to respect other humans, especially his parents and other authority figures. Then the results of Socrates saying will not become a reality. Unfortunately, there are parents of every generation who spoil their children to the point where they continue to be tyrants into adulthood. These children tend to be very ill-prepared for life as an adult.

"Be As You Wish To Seem."

This particular Socrates quote reminds me of the proverb in the Bible (in the book of Proverbs) that says "A man is what he thinks in his heart." Socrates hit the mark with "Be as you wish to seem." In other words, a man controls his destiny. If he thinks confidently and knows he is capable of success, then he will be successful in life. On the other hand, if he thinks negatively and puts himself down, he will likely fail in life as a result of his attitude. Individual self-talk is critical to one's development from youth up. Here again, parents play a critical role in encouraging their kids and nurturing them in a wholesome and loving environment. Complimenting their children and celebrating their successes will go a long way in helping their children think healthy thoughts, which will result in a healthy self-image.

Every person, when he comes of age and reaches the maturity level of thinking independently, becomes responsible for the way he thinks about himself. He has to make daily choices and try to choose the positive side of events. Life will throw you a curve, but you must want to take control of the adverse circumstance and come out on top. Life will knock a person down at times, but you need to get up and keep walking. You alone are responsible for your choices in life and must deal with the consequences of those choices. When you make the right decisions in life, the results will turn out favorably. Conversely, when you make negative choices, you will reap negative results in life. When a person thinks he will never fail, then he will never fail. The person who thinks he will fail, he will most likely fail in life.

I read about Ben Carson's life. He grew up in very difficult circumstances. His mother divorced early in his and his older brother's lives. His mother had a very limited third-grade education. Unfortunately, in the beginning of her unmarried life, she had to work very long hours, sometimes holding down 3 or 4 jobs at a time so that she could financially support her children. She eventually earned her GED and went to junior college, earning a degree. She became a fashion designer. She taught her sons that they could do whatever they put their minds to do in life. They could do it well and better than anyone else. His mother had the determination and the right attitude, and despite all of the disadvantages life gave her, she made something out of herself.

Ben had a negative mindset at first. He thought he was stupid and a poor student. He believed he was the worst student in his 5th-grade class. This belief was most likely due to the fact that he had no confidence in himself. His mother took the situation into her own hands, and made him start to do things that would help boost his confidence. She made him learn his times tables in math. She made him read two books and write book reports on those books. He couldn't go out and play until he finished his homework, read the books and wrote the reports, which were due on a weekly basis. He started reading and developed a real passion for the written word. It was then that her persistence began to pay off. She knew what it was like to feel like less of a person than others, and she knew what it took to break away from that attitude.

One day in 5th-grade, his science teacher held up a rock and asked anyone in the class what the rock was and to describe its properties. Ben recognized the rock, but waited to see if any of his classmates would raise their hands to answer the question. No one did, so Ben raised his hand, and everyone in class snickered. "Yes, Benjamin do you know?" Benjamin correctly identified the rock and went into great detail about its properties. "Correct Benjamin. Good insight and you named the rock correctly." The science teacher made a point to let the class know that Ben had answered the question right. From that day on, Ben Carson began to believe in himself and his classmates perceived him differently, as well. One and a half years later, Ben Carson was the number one student in his 6th-grade class.

That incident in the 5th grade forever changed his perception of his academic abilities, and all because his science teacher saw that potential in him. He was never again the worst student in class, but the top student. He went on to attend Yale and studied neurosurgery. He became one of the foremost neurosurgeons in the world, and perfected many neurological surgery procedures. At only 33 years of age, he became the youngest head of pediatric neurosurgery at John Hopkins University. He has written several bestsellers and has become one of the most celebrated neurosurgeons of all time. Ben believed in himself because his mother, his science teacher and many other mentors saw and nurtured his brilliant potential. So there is validity to Socrates statement: "Be as you wish to seem."

"The Hour Of Departure Has Arrived, And We Go Our Ways; I To Die, And You To Live. Which Is Better? Only God Knows."

The previous opinion begs the question of whether it is better to die before a person has reached his mission in life and accomplished all that he wanted to achieve? Conversely, is it better for a person to die or to live in unimaginable pain? Then this brings to mind the sensitive social issue whether a person on life support should have the plug pulled on them. Will the person be better off living in a vegetative state or would it be more humane to pull the plug on their life support and let him die? These questions and many others can be asked about this quote made by Socrates. From a Christian perspective, Paul the famous apostle asked one of his church congregations the same question in his biblical book, Philippians. He was asking them if it was better for him to die and go to be with Jesus forever in heaven? Or was it more feasible for him to stay on earth and continue pushing the Christian faith? Paul ended up living many more years and impacted the known world with his teachings about the Christian faith. So in his case, it was better for him to live because his writings still affect us a couple of thousands of years later. Back to the life support question, how many countless people have been in a life-threatening situation where their lives are hanging in the balance? Their loved ones agonize over the decision of whether to terminate their lives or keep them alive in a semi-dead state. Would it be better for these people to live or die? No human being knows that answer. Only the living God knows the answer to that ultimate question. But what if the loved one survives, and ends up making a significant contribution to the world that could save millions of other lives? Or what if the person, sad to say, went on to be a prolific serial killer and would take dozens of lives? Humans just cannot answer this question because they don't truly know whether it's better for that person to die or live. There is no certainty in what awaits us in death.

Again, I mention Ben Carson, the famous neurosurgeon who was referred to in an earlier section of this writing. A few times in his career he was called upon to perform very intricate brain surgeries that could kill or keep the patients alive. In one particular case, he performed a procedure to separate identical twins who were attached at the skull. One wrong incision and the boys would be dead. If the brain operation hadn't been performed, the twins would be permanently attached at the head, facing away from each other. The parents had to lift them up to sit them down because of their restricted mobility. There were many other simple actions the parents had to help the twins perform. Would life be worth living in such a limited state? What happens when the twins grow up and need support to live healthy lives? Who would be able to lift two fully grown twin men? Every time they needed to move from one location to another, or they had to sit down, how could this be done?

On the other hand, what if Dr. Carson had performed the surgery, and the twins had died? We would always wonder what their lives might have been like. What would they have accomplished in life? What if they accomplished nothing spectacular in life? Who is to know? Is it better for them to live or to die? Dr. Carson did perform the surgery, and successfully separated the twins. Only time will tell if it was better for them to die or to live. Either way, everyone deserves a chance at life. People's experiences throughout life will have a big impact on who they become. The point is that we never know what would have happened if someone lives or dies. A person could greatly affect the world or have no effect at all. One could die and exist in peace, or continuing to live could have brought more peace and happiness.

There is another case of a famous Christian music minister named Israel Houghton, who was conceived as the result of rape. His mother had a very emotional life-changing decision to make. Should she abort the child or let him come into the world? Would it be better to let him live and have the "rape stigma" hanging over his head? Or should she just end his life so no one would ever know he was the product of a horrendous rape? Surely if she aborted him, he would never know the difference. She would save herself a lot of uncomfortable questions and awkward social circumstances. So which is better - for him to die or live? She gave birth to him, and he has become one of the most influential Christian musicians in the world today. He has won many awards, and he is internationally known. He has impacted thousands upon thousands of lives with his music. So, in this case, it was better for him to live!

"One Who Is Injured Ought Not To Return To The Injury, For On No Account Can It Be Right To Do An Injustice; And It Is Not Right To

Return To An Injury, Or To Do Evil To Any Man, However Much We Have Suffered From Him."

Here Socrates is stating that revenge is wrong. No matter what that person has done to you, returning the injury is still an injustice. Many people in this world do evil things. They inflict pain and suffering on others. If you return the pain and suffering of the person who inflicted it in the first place, then you are making yourself equally as evil as that person. It is not relevant why you committed the action, only that you did, and no matter what that person has done, you are still committing an injustice. Instead of committing these evils, every person has the choice to walk away or to forgive. Showing this type of compassion may even help the person who has hurt you to change his ways, and rectify his past behavior. A more popular saying used today relaying this same message is "two wrongs don't make a right".

The biggest factor in following this standard is forgiveness. Anger is a basic human emotion, and when we get angry, we tend to take it out on those who have hurt us. Learning how to forgive is necessary for adopting this philosophy. If you cannot learn to forgive those who have hurt you, then you will never be able to move on from the pain of being wronged. The anger and grief can continue to have an effect on your everyday life. For example, if someone has hurt you in the past and you happen to cross paths with them again, if you have not forgiven and let go of the resentment, then it is likely that you will immediately get angry. This anger can ruin your day and even cause destructive behavior. However, if you have let go of your resentment, then you will be able to move on and continue to enjoy your day with nothing but a brief, painful memory. Many experts in psychology agree that continuing to hold onto anger and seek out revenge can lead to self-destructive behavior that will, in the end, cause you more harm than it will to the person you have fixated on. This scenario is seen many times in relationships. If a person is hurt by their partner and they feel the need to get revenge, then it sets the relationship on a destructive path that leads to both parties suffering more than necessary.

To apply this philosophy in your everyday life, always remember that it is important to learn to forgive and not to seek out revenge against those who have wronged you. An important step in learning to forgive others is learning to forgive yourself. This idea means you have to forgive yourself for any behavior you had that may have put you in a position to get hurt in the first place. For example, if you were an abused child, you may blame yourself for your abuse by making yourself believe it was due to your bad behavior. The self-blame will cause the blame you put on other people to be even stronger. However, learning to forgive yourself can allow you to forgive others as well. To learn to forgive others, you may also need to learn to forgive yourself for any harm you may have done to others. If you have wronged someone and cannot forgive yourself, then you definitely will not be willing to forgive others for hurting you. You also might need to forgive yourself for any harm that you have inflicted upon yourself. Doing these things can help you to ease yourself of any guilt or rage that you have toward yourself for things you have done. In turn, you will be more open to letting go of your resentment toward others which will lead you to make wiser choices on how to deal with the hurt associated with being wronged. This way you can redirect that energy into positive things.

When forgiving others instead of seeking revenge, it may not be a good thing to completely forget the injury. Another saying that comes to mind, in this case, is "forgive and forget". I It is nearly impossible to forgive completely, and you may never be able to completely forget. It is okay to remember how hurt you were or even to experience some lingering emotions. These emotions may protect you from allowing the same things to happen to you over and over. As important as it is for you not to seek revenge on others, it is equally important for you to protect yourself from further damage. You can do this by letting go of the resentment and moving on, but also remember what lead you to get hurt in the first place so that you can take preventative steps to avoid it happening again. By being aware, you can change patterns and improve your relationships instead of destroying them further.

Society needs people to adopt this quote in their everyday lives. In current society, revenge is something people get very fixated on. For example, capital punishment is something that is still being practiced in some places. Killing someone in return for killing does not rectify the situation, and it does not teach the offender any lessons. There is no redemption with the finality of capital punishment. People need forgiveness from others as much as they need to forgive others. Those who have wronged someone can learn a lesson from it, but if revenge is sought out against them, then it makes it difficult for them to forgive themselves. Lack of forgiveness can lead them into more destructive behavior, and it continues the cycle. A person who is injured and chooses not to return the injury will likely find more peace than those who choose to return the injury.

"If A Man Is Proud Of His Wealth, He Should Not Be Praised Until It Is Known How He Employs It."

This Socrates quote is saying that it does not matter how much money you have. What matters is what you do with the money you have. There are a lot of wealthy people who do nothing useful with their money. They spend it on material items that do not matter. Other rich people do great things with their money that positively impact others. They donate to the right causes and help to change the world, and they still live a financially comfortable life. The one who does good things with the money is the one who deserves the praise because they are doing things that matter. The one who is doing nothing good with the money does not deserve praise because he is only using it for things that will not make any difference in the world. It is important to choose how you use your wealth wisely because so many people can be impacted by how the wealthy choose to spend.

The important concept in this quote to remember is that it is imperative how you use your wealth. Greed and gluttony will not only have adverse effects on you, but also on society. For example, Andrew Carnegie was a man who created a steel production company. He made his employees work very long hours, with only one day off per year, and he paid them very low wages. As a result, the thousands of men who worked for him suffered through poverty while Carnegie became wealthy. His greed impacted not only his workers, but the entire economy. On the other hand, there are people like Oprah Winfrey, who have dedicated their wealth to charities, and helping others. With her generosity, Oprah has saved many lives and improved the lives of many people in crisis. Andrew Carnegie is the prime example of someone who should not be praised for his wealth. Oprah Winfrey should be praised for using her wealth to impact the world in a very positive way. The way you use your money will become your legacy. Today, Carnegie is referred to as a villain, and rightfully so. He is used as a cautionary tale in history books, and he is the reason we have labor laws. Oprah Winfrey is celebrated for all of the great things she has done.

It is not difficult to apply this in your everyday life. If you are lucky enough to be wealthy, then you just need to put some of what you have into doing things that could help society. Greed becomes a habit with many rich people, and breaking that habit is as easy as making charitable donations to some causes that inspire passion within you. Do things with your wealth that will better our society, and you will benefit from it because you get to live in a better society as a result. For example, if the wealthy company owners do things that will help our economy, then more people will be able to afford the products the company produces. In turn, that wealth will likely return to the generous business owners in the form of increased sales. Another benefit would be the praise the company gets for being generous, which will also increase sales because people like buying from companies with good reputations.

Many studies have been conducted over the last few years that suggest using wealth to help others can be surprisingly good for your well-being. It is said that generosity can even lengthen your lifespan. Using your money to make a difference is not only good for society and the economy, but it is good for your health. All of the material things you could buy are much less likely to have benefits like that.

If you are not someone who has monetary wealth, it is likely that you are wealthy in other ways. Wealth comes in many forms. Just think of anything that you have plenty of and consider the good things you could do with some of what you don't need. You can still use whatever wealth you may have and apply this philosophy to your life. If you have an abundant garden, you can share food with those in need, or if you have good health, you can volunteer your time and energy to local charities. Many of us are not monetarily wealthy, but it can still make a difference. No matter what type of wealth you are sharing, it does make a difference. In turn, you may receive praise for your wealth, even if you don't have a lot of money. Applying this quote to your life only requires you to give some of whatever you have in excess.

Society needs people to apply this philosophy to their lives. Greed is not uncommon, and the world's wealth is shared by a minuscule percentage of the world's population. It is critical to society that wealthy people start to distribute their wealth by donating some of it to those in need. There are so many great charities out there that need donations. Many individuals in crisis aren't getting the medicines, food, shelter, and other things they may need to survive. If all those people who have more than enough, donated just a small portion of their money, food, or whatever else they may have in excess, it could have a substantial impact on our economy. Not only would our economy benefit, but so would those who are donating to others, and those who are receiving the donations.

"Employ Your Time In Improving Yourself By Other Men's Writings, So That You Shall Gain Easily What Others Have Labored Hard For."

Here Socrates is stating that learning from those who have been successful will help you get the things you desire quicker. Every successful person had to go through a series of experiences, both good and bad, to get where they got. Many successful people also write about how they got there. Many books record how those people succeeded and failures they experienced along the way. By reading these materials, we can learn from the success of others, and it can teach us how to become successful ourselves. Those who were the first to succeed in their field worked very hard to get there. They likely failed many times. The people who want to follow can read other men's writings to avoid some of the pitfalls that may have caused the men to fail. By learning from the mistakes of others, you can become successful quicker and easier. The knowledge of others can lay out a path for success.

Self-improvement is the central concept everyone should take away from this quote and apply to their lives. Life is one big learning experience, and everybody should take any opportunity they are given to learn more about what they can do to make themselves better. The knowledge and experiences you can learn from others is the most valuable type of knowledge available. You can educate yourself about the mistakes that have been made by others so you can avoid making the same mistakes. To live successfully, people should remember to keep on learning along the way to avoid losing what they have gained. Every person has flaws that they would like to change, and self-improvement is about always working to make these changes. One of the best ways to gain the knowledge necessary to do this is through books. There are countless biographies and autobiographies available to us today, and there is so much to be gained from them. For example, if you are an alcoholic, then read a book about a former alcoholic. Getting this information can help you discover how the alcoholic overcame his illness. You can find out exactly what works and what doesn't. With a little bit of work, you can imitate his success. Using these methods to improve yourself will make it more likely that success will be your result.

Bringing about change in life is as simple as picking up a book. Just start by reading books about people who have faced obstacles similar to the ones you face in your everyday life. It is likely that you will come across a few that you can relate to very closely. Use the knowledge in these books, and apply it to the obstacles you face. The books you can relate to should not only teach you how to be successful in what you are trying to do, but some of them may even ignite a need to change. Inspirational reading will motivate you to put what you have learned to good use. There are many self-improvement books out there, and most of these books are very motivating. They will help drive you to make a change. For example, The Secret by Rhonda Byrne will teach you the power of positive thinking. There are many claims about how this book has changed lives. It has helped people get their dream job, or overcome depression, and many other things. Not only will the book inspire you, but the testimonies of others will also help you to continue using the book to improve yourself and your life. This book is not the only book out there like this. There are thousands of self-help books out there that cover every topic from overcoming addiction, to being a strong leader. So pick the book that suits your needs and start reading.

The hardest part of this process is likely to be applying what you've learned and using it to your advantage. Making changes within yourself can be a difficult process. You have to find a way to make this new way of thinking or acting come naturally to you. For example, a pessimist usually thinks negatively. To become more of a positive thinker, a person would have to retrain their mind to think positively. Changing the way you think does not come naturally, and it can take work. Luckily most of these books either outline exactly how a person made the changes by explaining what works and what doesn't or they explain how to get back on the path to self-improvement if you have taken a step in the wrong direction. Changing is not easy, but anyone can do it with a bit of determination.

Today, so many people seem to be stuck in their ways. This quote should be used by those people because they have developed a habit of refusing to learn, and refusing to improve themselves. Due to this, many people seem to be making the same mistakes over and over. For example, many people who end up in prison, seem to keep going back. If they found a way to stop the cycle, it would result in a better life for themselves, and thus they may have hurt by continuing to do whatever negative things they are repeatedly doing. By picking up a book, everyone can learn something new and improve themselves so that they can break the habit of making these mistakes. If everyone began working on improving their attitudes and lives, then it would change society for the better.

"Worthless People Live Only To Eat And Drink; People Full Of Worth Eat And Drink To Live."

Those who only live to survive do not live meaningful lives. Those who do what they have to so that they can survive to be able to achieve other things, do live meaningful lives. Some people simply survive so they eat, drink and sleep, but they do not strive for better things. They do not improve themselves. These people do not accomplish anything in life, and they make no impact on the world. On the other hand, some people eat and drink to survive so that they can do greater things with their lives. These people better themselves and accomplish goals. They do make a difference in the world. What you do throughout your life measures your worth. If you impact the lives of others and make changes in the world, then you have lived with purpose and made a meaningful life that is full of worth.

Making a meaningful life is important to each person's physical and mental wellbeing. Being productive will help you to live a healthier life, and it will make you feel good about yourself. No matter what you choose to do, productivity will help you achieve the benefits of having a meaningful life. Living meaningfully also means you get to experience more. Your way of living a meaningful life could mean you get to experience traveling the world, or it could mean watching your children grow, either way, you get to experience things that will give you pleasant memories and good feelings that can help improve your health and make you feel like you have a purpose. Living a productive life also means making connections and building relationships. Those people who you build relationships with will learn from how you live. Those with purpose, inspire people around them and drive them to bring meaning into their lives as well. Everyone should strive to do something in life. They should set goals and achieve them. Hard work and stress many come with it, but in the end, the benefits will be worth the effort.

Bringing meaningfulness into your life can be complicated or simple, depending on what it is you choose to do, but the process remains the same. First, you must know what's important to you. Find your values and stick with them. Go after something you will enjoy. Whether you choose to be a doctor or a model, make sure it is something that makes you feel passionate. Be aware of your actions, and make sure you are doing things that bring you closer to your goals, not further from them. Many people end up on self-destructive paths by not being self-aware. Put your relationships with others before material items. Material things are easily replaced; people can't be replaced. Be kind and thoughtful toward others and find ways to donate time or money to help improve society. Whether you are giving a dollar to the homeless man holding a sign or spending weekends volunteering at the animal shelter, you are doing something to improve society. Set goals and work toward them. Write your goals down and stride toward achieving them daily. Doing these things will give your life meaning in one way or another. You might impact other people's lives for the better, or have a positive impact on a cause.

Having a meaningful life can come with stress. Those who live only to eat and drink most likely do not have much stress because they do not have things they are passionate enough to work for. For example, if you choose to have a family, then you have a lot of meaning, but, it comes with good and bad. Raising children can be joyous, but it can also be incredibly hard sometimes. The same can be said for almost any path with meaning. Achieving things can take hard work and determination. There will likely be moments of failure, but anyone who wishes to have meaning in their lives must keep pushing for success, despite a few setbacks here and there.

Society is in need of people with more determination to do something meaningful with their lives. So many people are comfortable living off social security handouts from their family. People like this have no commitment to become self-sufficient. They do not have the motivation to improve themselves and make strides towards a more meaningful life. This attitude hurts our economy and causes others to have to forfeit more of their earnings in the form of taxes. If more people would eat and drink to live, versus living to eat and drink, then we would have a more productive society which would improve our world in many ways. We would also have a happier community that makes more progress in the changes that we need to have a more functional world.

In Summary

The wisdom of philosophers from our past is unmatched by anything I've seen. Socrates was a Greek philosopher in ancient times. The famous Plato was not surprisingly a student of his. His wisdom is used as a basis for Western logic and morals. Socrates believed that his work should improve society, and he taught his work to many. Improving society is precisely what his work has done. He was renown for his intelligence and intuitive way of thinking. He understood what it would take to succeed in many aspects of life, and he graciously shared this with anyone who was willing to listen. Socrates quotes are a guide to finding success, happiness, and prosperity for anyone who is willing to follow his words. Unfortunately, his wisdom is only known by few in modern times. Many people are not as aware of Socrates as they once were. His life-changing quotes have fallen so far into the background, that they are no longer common knowledge. If his work were taught more in today's society, we likely wouldn't have many of the ongoing issues we face today. Each one of these quotes applies to modern times just as well as they did in the past.

Each and every one of these quotes can be used as a lesson on how to live a happier life with more value. The quotes provide a vast variety of eye-opening concepts. Some provide knowledge on how to use books about the experiences of others to gain success, as well as how to use your wealth in a praiseworthy manner. Each quote teaches a different concept that most people today have not even considered. Socrates quotes should spark a realization in everyone on how to improve at least one aspect of their lives. So many people are struggling with illness and poverty in the world today. Many others are struggling at their own hand due to destructive behaviors. Socrates's wisdom could ignite a change in our world if it were taught more values.

Socrates's wisdom is something that everyone should adopt. Each of these quotes teaches a valuable lesson that should be applied in everyone's life. If more people would adopt these quotes, then our world would change drastically for the better. People would be more driven, and compassionate. Greed would not plague our society to the point where so many people go without basic needs. People would be wiser in how they live their lives. Negativity would not be as prevalent in our world. It would be the closest thing to world peace that we could ever see. In today's times, those like Socrates who have useful knowledge are not as renown or celebrated as they once were. Many have lost their moral compass. If more people could bring old and new wisdom into their lives, then everyone could live more fulfilling lives, and our society would be less likely to suffer anymore.

Conclusion

It is not living that matters but living rightly. – Socrates

I hope this book was able to help you understand Socrates' a little better, especially in his philosophic theories such as living a virtuous life and caring for the soul. I hope that you will contemplate on these lessons and live accordingly to them.

Finally, if you enjoyed this book, please take the time to share your thoughts and post a review on Amazon. It'd be greatly appreciated!

Click HERE to Leave a Review for this Book!

Instant Access to Free Book Package!

As a thank you for the purchase of this book, I want to offer you some more material. We collaborate with multiple other authors specializing in various fields. We have best-selling, master writers in history, biographies, DIY projects, home improvement, arts & crafts and much more! **We make a promise to you to deliver at least 4 books a week in different genres, a value of $20-30, for FREE!**

All you need to do is sign up your email here at http://nextstopsuccess.net/freebooks/ to join our Book Club. You will get weekly notification for more free books, courtesy of the First Class Book Club.

As a special thank you, we don't want you to wait until next week for these 4 free books. We want to give you 4 **RIGHT NOW**.

Here's what you will be getting:

1. A fitness book called "BOSU Workout Routine Made Easy!"
2. A book on Jim Rohn, a master life coach: "The Best of Jim Rohn: Lessons for Life Changing Success"
3. A detailed biography on Conan O'Brien, a favorite late night TV show host.
4. A World War 2 Best Selling box set (2 books in 1!): "The Third Reich: Nazi Rise & Fall + World War 2: The Untold Secrets of Nazi Germany".

To get instant access to this free ebook package (a value of $25), and weekly free material, all you need to do is click the link below:

http://nextstopsuccess.net/freebooks/

Add us on Facebook: First Class Book Club

Made in the USA
San Bernardino, CA
25 May 2018